# MEDITATIONS
# ON FIRST PHILOSOPHY

The Library of Liberal Arts

# MEDITATIONS ON FIRST PHILOSOPHY

RENÉ DESCARTES

Translated, with an introduction, by
LAURENCE J. LAFLEUR

The Library of Liberal Arts
*published by*

Macmillan Publishing Company
New York
Collier Macmillan Publishers
London

Rene Descartes: 1596 - 1650

**MEDITATIONS ON FIRST PHILOSOPHY** was originally
published in 1641

. . . . . . . . . . . . . . . . . . .

Macmillan Publishing Company
866 Third Avenue
New York, New York, 10022
Collier Macmillan Canada, Inc.

PRINTING 36 37 38 39 40    YEAR    3 4 5 6

ISBN 0-02-367170-X

# CONTENTS

· · · · · · · · · · · · · · · · ·

## MEDITATIONS
## ON FIRST PHILOSOPHY

# NOTE ON THE TEXT

The translation of the *Meditations* is taken from three sources: the second Latin edition of 1642, which was the first one printed from Descartes' own manuscript and under his own supervision, the first French translation of 1647 by the Duc de Luynes, but read and approved by Descartes, and the second French translation by Clerselier. An attempt has been made in this translation to integrate these three versions into one complete and accurate edition by the use of brackets and parentheses. The reader may, by omitting the parentheses and brackets, have a translation which contains all ideas in the three versions. By omitting bracketed material, he will have a translation essentially that of the original Latin, and by omitting material in parentheses, that of the first French edition.

( )  indicates where the Latin adds a word or phrase not found in the French.

[ ]  indicates where the first French version adds a word or phrase not found in the Latin.

( )[ ]  indicates where the two versions differ. The Latin enclosed in the parentheses; the first French enclosed in square brackets. A connective such as "and" or "or" is occasionally supplied and the brackets and parentheses overlap so as to include it.

[( )]  indicates material occurring for the first time in the second French edition.

The numbers enclosed in brackets and parentheses refer to the corresponding pages in the French and Latin texts of the Adam and Tannery editions. The numbers enclosed in parentheses refer to the second Latin text; the numbers enclosed in brackets, to the first French text.

# INTRODUCTION

### Concerning the Translation

This is the second in a series of translations of Descartes' more important works, the first being the *Discourse on Method*, presented in the same series as the present work. The reader is referred to it for a discussion of Descartes' place in history, his influence in the development of modern science, and his attitude toward religion.

The *Meditations* offer us two types of problems: those of translation and those of interpretation. The most basic problem of translation arises from the multiplicity of texts in both Latin and French which have some claim to rank as originals, and which, in view of the importance of this work, the translator must take into account.

The first version was in Latin: *Meditationes de Prima Philosophia* appeared in Paris in 1641. It contained a "Letter to the Faculty of Theology at Paris," a "Preface from the Author to the Reader," an "Index," a "Synopsis," an "Extract from the King's Privilege," the six "Meditations," and six sets of "Objections and Replies." A second Latin edition was published in Amsterdam the following year; it omitted the "Index" and "Extract from the King's Privilege," and added a seventh set of "Objections and Replies" and a "Letter to P. Dinet."

The "Fifth Objections and Replies" were by Gassendi, who in 1644 published, under the title *Disquisitio Metaphysica*, his original objections, Descartes' replies, and a further discussion by himself, to which the original *Meditationes* were added as an appendix. This volume did not, of course, include the other "Objections and Replies," nor any of the introductory material.

In 1647 there appeared the first French edition, translated from the first Latin by the Duc de Luynes and Clerselier, the former doing the "Meditations" proper, the latter the "Objections and Replies." Of the introductory material, the "Preface" and "Index" were omitted, and a "Notice from the Publisher" added. As Gassendi had claimed in his *Disquisitio* that his "Objections" had been published without his approval, Descartes did not wish these "Fifth Objections" to be used. Consequently, he had a summary of the *Disquisitio* prepared for him, since he found the original too long, and to this he wrote a reply in the form of a "Letter to Clerselier." This letter was prefaced by two "Notices," one by the author, the other by the translator, and appeared between the fourth and sixth sets of "Objections." After this substitution, however, Clerselier had a change of heart and added his translation of the "Fifth Objections," placing it at the end, after the "Sixth Objections." This was the only part of the French translation not read and approved by Descartes.

In 1650 there appeared the fourth Latin edition, differing from the second in omitting the "Fifth Objections and Replies" and substituting a translation from the French of the "Letter to Clerselier." A "Letter to Voetius" and "Notae in Programma" were also added after the "Letter to P. Dinet," with which they have a logical connection. A number of further Latin editions were taken without change from this fourth edition.

In 1661, eleven years after the death of Descartes, Clerselier published the second French edition. In addition to the contents of the first French edition, this contained the "Preface," the "Seventh Objections and Replies," and the "Letter to P. Dinet." More important, Clerselier corrected the Duc de Luynes' translation of the "Meditations" proper. Finally, in 1673, René Fédé brought out the third French edition, substituting his own "Notice from the Editor" for the "Notice from the Publishers" of the second edition, supplying a "Table of Contents" instead of the "Synopsis," and providing cross-references throughout.

Of this material, which should be chosen as the basis of a new translation into English? As far as the "Objections and Replies" are concerned, as well as the "Preface" and other subsidiary items, the problem is complicated by the fact that some of these are not found in all the editions. But leaving this aside for the moment, a text of the "Meditations" proper must be selected for translation.

Of the Latin editions, Descartes appears to have had no personal connection with the third and later editions; the first was printed in Paris while Descartes was in Holland and was taken, not from his manuscript, but from a copy. The second edition, which does not vary much from the first, was published at a time and place such that Descartes could, and probably did, supervise its publication. The second Latin edition was therefore selected for the Adam and Tannery text. The pagination of this text, as found in Volume VII, is indicated in our English translation by numbers in parentheses.

The first French translation was read and approved by Descartes; the second appeared about eleven years after his death. Naturally enough, the first was selected by Adam and Tannery, and that selection is followed here. The pagination, as found in Volume IX, is indicated here by numbers in square brackets. But unlike Adam and Tannery, the present translator does not think that the second French edition should be entirely ignored.

Let us examine, for a moment, the characteristics of the Duc de Luynes' translation. Technically speaking, it is a very poor one. In addition to the occasional mistakes that may be expected in any translation, adjectives and adjectival expressions are frequently attached to the wrong noun, and adverbs and adverbial expressions are similarly transposed. In the seventeenth century, be it remembered, a very degenerate form of Latin was in use, and a carelessness of grammar was fairly typical. In this case it would appear that the Duc de Luynes paid little or no attention to grammar and arranged his sentences by "the light of nature," or rather by his understanding of Descartes' meaning. It speaks well for this understanding that the French translation, despite its variations from the Latin original, seems quite as true to Descartes' thought as the latter. We must also remember that the translation was read and approved by the author.

Now, while the Duc de Luynes was preparing his translation, Clerselier not only translated the much more voluminous "Objections and Replies," and was in frequent communication with Descartes on this subject, but also prepared his own translation of the "Meditations" proper. It is therefore quite possible that Descartes had seen part of Clerselier's translation, which was only published in 1661, or that Clerselier had discussed some of it with him; or that a discussion of the text written by the Duc de Luynes, or of his own text of the "Objections," gave some authority to the later work of Clerselier.

I do not maintain this as being the actual truth, but the relationship between Descartes and Clerselier was such that we cannot treat the latter's translation as though it had been originally undertaken after the death of Descartes.

Very well, then, we now have three texts that carry authority for us; how shall we decide among them? Fortunately, there are no major differences, and most of the minor ones are due merely to the different modes of expression in French and Latin. Where there are discrepancies the translator has felt free to use whichever text seemed to him to produce the best English translation. Other things being equal, the Latin text is preferred to the French where the thought is not affected, on the assumption that Descartes himself would not have been concerned with trivial differences. This is particularly true in cases where the second French edition agrees with the Latin. When the meaning in one language is ambiguous, the version of the other language is considered decisive, except *quatenus* (p. 14, l. 7), which appears to be mistranslated into French as *en tant que* [p. 10, l. 31]. Where the Latin adds a thought that is not found in the French, the word or phrase is enclosed in parentheses; to prevent confusion, the few parentheses in the original have been incorporated into the main text. On the other hand, where the first French version adds a word or phrase that is not found in the Latin, that material is enclosed in square brackets. Where the two versions differ, the Latin version is enclosed in parentheses, the first French in square brackets. In the interest of fluency, a connective, such as "and" or "or," is occasionally supplied and brackets and parentheses overlap so as to include it. Material occurring for the first time in the second French edition is enclosed in both brackets and parentheses.

An invented example involving all these devices will serve to explain this system more clearly. Let the Latin read: "Let us suppose that a bit of wax is presented to my eye." Let the first French version be: "A bit of wax is presented clearly to my sense of sight." Let the second French version be: "A bit of wax is presented clearly and immediately to my sense of sight." Then the English translation would read as follows: "(Let us suppose that) a bit of wax is presented [clearly (and immediately)] to my (eye [or) sense of sight]." Of course no actual instance is as complex as this. Notice that the reader may ignore both parentheses and brackets, and have an English translation which contains all ideas given in any of the three versions. If he wishes to have a translation which is essentially that of the original Latin, he need only omit all material included in brackets. Omitting the material enclosed in parentheses gives a translation of the first French edition. It is intended that all three methods of reading should result in a fluent English text.

Let us now turn to the subsidiary material. A "Letter to the Faculty of Theology at Paris" is found in all editions, and has likewise been included in the present translation. A "Notice from the Publisher" of the first French edition, which appeared in both the first and second French editions, and a "Notice from the Editor" of the third French edition, which appeared in that edition, were both omitted from the translation, since neither of them appeared in the Latin and since they are not the work of Descartes. A "Preface from the Author to the Reader" occurs in all editions except the first French, and is here translated, based equally on the second Latin and the second French editions, with brackets indicating material from the latter. An "Index," which appeared in the first Latin only, and a "Table of Contents," which appeared only in the third French edition, have not been included. However, a "Synopsis" ("*Abrégé*"), which appeared in all editions except the third French, has been translated in the same way as the six "Meditations," that is, by indicating the variations in the texts of both the Latin and French versions. There was no occasion to translate the "Extract from the King's Privilege," essentially a copyright, which appeared in the French editions and in the first Latin.

A different problem was posed by the "Objections." There are seven sets of these, each one followed by Descartes' "Replies," in addition to Gassendi's further "Instances" and Descartes' answer in the "Letter to Clerselier." There are also Descartes' and Clerselier's "Notices," the "Letter to P. Dinet," the "Letter to Voetius," and "Notae in Programma." The value of this material was not questioned; its bulk alone forbade its inclusion in this volume. Excluding the "Instances," which were never published by Descartes and only appeared in Gassendi's *Disquisitio Metaphysica,* and excluding also the "Letter to Voetius" and "Notae in Programma," which are only tenuously connected with the main work, the remaining material is more than seven times the length of the "Meditations" proper. It must be left, therefore, to a future occasion to offer extracts from the "Objections and Replies" in a separate volume.

### Some Problems of Meaning

It is noticeable that Descartes is much more addicted to the use of double adjectives in French than in Latin, and his translator either shows the same tendency or else Descartes himself corrected the translation accordingly. Now it is quite natural for any translation to show such a duplication, since two words may be needed to convey in a second language all the implications of a single word in the original. Yet in the greater number of cases the purpose seems to be purely stylistic, as confirmed by the treatment of adverbs, phrases, and sentence structure generally. Although the present translator has not allowed this opinion to interfere with the accuracy of his translation, it does not seem to him that an effort to understand the meaning of individual words in Descartes is well directed. Descartes' thought is always clear, even if the use of words is sometimes inconsistent.

The most frequent example of this duplication of adjectives is the phrase "clear and distinct," which occurs in both the Latin and French. Descartes himself explains the meaning of these terms in the *Principles of Philosophy,* Part I, Principle XLV:

> I call "clear" that which is present and manifest to an attentive mind; just as we say we clearly see objects when they are present, when they act sufficiently strongly (to affect us), and when our eyes are turned to look at them. And I call that "distinct" which is so precise and different from all other things that it contains nothing which does not appear manifestly to one who considers it properly.

While this meaning of the term is evidently in Descartes' mind at some points in the *Meditations,* he does not adhere to it consistently. This is evidenced by the fact that the word "distinct" in the Latin version sometimes becomes "clear" in the French and at other times "clear and distinct"; and similarly for the word "clear."

One of the most confusing points is Descartes' use of psychological terms. "Mind" and "soul" are usually synonymous and are declared to be so. "Thought" sometimes means mind, or it may be used to refer to any mental process, though most frequently to conception. Conception may also be referred to as "perception," particularly in the Latin, or as "intellection," "judgment," or "knowledge"; while perception is sometimes referred to as "sensation," and so forth. The meaning is generally clear in either language, though the French terminology tends to be more consistent than the Latin. Some effort has been made, within the limits appropriate for a translation, to make the English version somewhat more consistent than either the Latin or the French.

A term frequently used in the *Meditations* is "lumen naturalis" or "lumière naturelle." Although the literal translation would be "the natural light" or "the light of nature," the translator was strongly tempted to use "natural insight" as the English version, believing it would more nearly convey Descartes' meaning to the modern reader than would the more literal translation. But because of the common use of "lumen naturalis" in the Renaissance period and the frequent occurrence of the literal English translation in the literature of the day, it was decided to concur in the tradition.

To Descartes, as to writers of the Renaissance generally, "the light of nature" was, in part, a mental faculty given to man by God for the immediate apprehension of truth. The concept is somewhat similar to the English idea of conscience, with three exceptions. First, conscience is thought of as operating in ethical matters only, whereas the light of nature is primarily concerned with intellectual truths, though doubtless not debarred from operating in the ethical field as well. The second difference is that the light of nature is thought of as natural—that is, as being part of the essence of man—so that while one hears occasionally of a man "without a conscience," a man without the light of nature would be as inconceivable to Descartes as a triangle without sides. And the third difference is that conscience is thought of as a mental faculty whose objective ground is the will of God, not mediated through the nonhuman part of the universe. The light of nature, however, is part of objective nature as well as of God and man; the human faculty has as its objective ground the necessary rationality of the God-created universe.

In the Sixth Meditation, Descartes refers to that part of the brain in which "sensus communis" is located; or, literally, where common sense is found. But common sense does not here have its usual meaning; rather, it refers to what a modern psychologist would call the sensory areas of the brain. Since to use this equivalence might attribute to Descartes too great a knowledge of contemporary psychology, the translation is made to read literally: "where the senses in common have their seat."

### The Older Descartes

The *Discourse on Method, Dioptrics, Meteorology,* and *Geometry* were published in 1637, but had been written quite some time earlier, some of it at least ten years earlier. The *Meditations* were published in 1641, but although some of it was no doubt written earlier, probably none of it antedated the *Discourse.* Thus the four-year interval in the time of publication of the two works represents a much longer interval in the time of writing; and although there are very few differences in the doctrines proclaimed by Descartes before and after this interval, there is a world of difference in his attitude.

Descartes is not only the father of modern philosophy, of modern mathematics, and of modern physics, optics, meteorology, and science generally, but also the child of the Middle Ages. The ideas of Aristotle and of Mediaeval philosophy are so deeply ingrained in him that they are never really questioned; they govern the pattern of his thinking even when he does not consciously admit them and they are openly espoused during the development of his thought as the dictates of the light of nature. So in Descartes there were two competing tendencies: he was at once the progressive, or rather the radical intellectual rebel, ready to break away from Mediaevalism and the Church to lay the foundation of a new philosophy and to build his hopes for the future of mankind on the development of science in general and of medicine in particular; and at the same time he was the conservative, educated in the Mediaeval tradition by the monks of the Jesuit order.

It is a matter of common experience that older persons tend more to conservatism; for this reason alone it is not strange that the Descartes of 1641 should have been more conservative than the Descartes of 1637 and earlier. But there was a more telling reason for the change. The Descartes of 1637 and before, while not actually unknown, had published nothing. His teachers, friends, and acquaintances recognized his abilities and expected great things of him, but as much can be said of countless men in every generation. Would this expectation be fulfilled? Born in 1596, Descartes was not so young any more, and doubts may have arisen in the minds of his friends and perhaps even in his own. Descartes tells us himself, in the *Discourse,* that someone had circulated the rumor that his philosophy was completed. His situation was like that later described by Daudet: he ran the risk of being compared to *"lou fusiou de mestre Gervaï,"* and like Daudet's hero Tartarin, he willingly faced dangers to avoid losing not only his reputation but also his self-esteem.

In 1641, the situation was completely changed; the writings of 1637 had achieved a tremendous *éclat* and had established Descartes' reputation throughout Europe. He was honored and deferred to in philosophic, scientific, and theological circles. From having everything to gain and nothing to lose, his position had changed to that of having nothing to gain and everything to lose. Why antagonize the Church, the most powerful force in Europe, and the most terrible adversary?

So Descartes' later work shows important differences from his earlier. Not that his philosophy had changed, but the emphasis had shifted. Those issues in which he was in agreement with the Church were stressed, and the points of disagreement completely overlooked. Certainly there are no passages in the *Meditations* comparable to those in the *Discourse on Method,* in which Descartes' allegiance to Church doctrine is proclaimed in what seems, to the present translator at least, an unmistakably ironic vein. The choice of language also is indicative; Descartes now writes in Latin, the language of the Church, of the Middle Ages, of the conservative intellectuals; instead of in French, as formerly, with the consequent appeal to fewer clergy and more lay readers.

In science, too, the change is notable. The later Descartes has few new theories to offer—nothing certainly to compare with his great fecundity of earlier years—and even these are largely developments of ideas that appeared in his earlier work. Of his later theories, the most important is the statement of what is now known as Newton's first law of motion. Next in importance is the theory of vortices, which was scientifically inaccurate and apparently conceived in the hope of reconciling Galileo's concept of the solar system with the *homo*-centric position of the Church, by means of a primitive theory of relativity. At the same time Descartes affirms the nonexistence of void, which logically leads to the conclusion that the propagation of light is instantaneous, in contradiction to his earlier view.

Thus the Descartes of the *Meditations* is both philosophically and scientifically less advanced than the Descartes of the *Discourse on Method*. Yet, while the *Method* is historically more significant, the *Meditations* have been traditionally rated Descartes' most important philosophic work, and from the point of view of philosophical content rather than historical significance, this is undoubtedly the case. The *Meditations* contain the most thorough exposition and defense of Descartes' philosophy, and it is in this work that he most clearly indicates the presuppositions, mainly taken from scholasticism, upon which his reasoning is based. Whether the reader agrees or disagrees with a particular argument, he is sure to find the reading of the *Meditations* a challenging experience and one of the most rewarding studies in all the great literature of philosophy.

LAURENCE J. LAFLEUR

# SELECTED BIBLIOGRAPHY

## DESCARTES' MAJOR WORKS

Discours de la méthode (1637).
Dioptrique (1637).
La Géométrie (1637).
Les Météores (1637).
Meditationes de prima philosophia (1641).
Principia philosophiae (1644).
Oeuvres de Descartes, publiées par Charles Adam et Paul Tannery sous les auspices du Ministère de l'instruction publique. Paris, 1897-1913.

## COLLATERAL READING

Balz, A. G., *Descartes and the Modern Mind.* Yale University, 1952.
———, *Cartesian Studies.* Columbia University, 1951.
Brunschwicg, Léon, *Descartes et Pascal, lecteurs de Montaigne.* Paris and New York, 1944.
———, *René Descartes.* Paris, 1937.
Cajori, Florian, *Ce que Newton doit à Descartes.* Paris, 1926.
Cresson, André, *Descartes; sa vie, son oeuvre.* Paris, 1942.
Fischer, Kuno, *Descartes and His School.* London, 1887.
Gibson, A. Boyce, *The Philosophy of Descartes.* London, 1932.
Gilson, Étienne, *Le rôle de la pensée médiévale dans la formation du système cartésien.* Paris, 1930.
———, *La doctrine cartésienne de la liberté et la théologie.* Paris, 1913.
Iverach, James, *Descartes, Spinoza and the New Philosophy.* New York, 1904.
Jascolevich, Alejandro A., *Three Conceptions of Mind. Their Bearing on the Denaturalization of the Mind in History.* New York, 1926.
Keeling, S. V., *Descartes.* London, 1934.

Kemp Smith, Norman, *New Studies in the Philosophy of Descartes*. London, 1953.

Laporte, Jean Marie Frédéric, *Le rationalisme de Descartes*. Paris, 1945.

Lévy-Bruhl, L., *History of Modern Philosophy in France*. Chicago, 1899.

Maritain, Jacques, *Three Reformers: Luther, Descartes, Rousseau*. New York, 1937.

Mouy, Paul, *Le développement de la physique cartésienne, 1646-1712*. Paris, 1934.

Roy, Jean H., *L'imagination selon Descartes*. Paris, 1944.

Scott, J. F., *The Scientific Work of René Descartes*. London, 1953.

Tellier, Auguste, *Descartes et la médecine*. Paris, 1928.

Vartanian, A., *Diderot and Descartes*. Princeton University, 1953.

Versfeld, Marthinus, *An Essay on the Metaphysics of Descartes*. London, 1940.

# THE MEDITATIONS ON FIRST PHILOSOPHY

*In Which the Existence of God and the
[Real] Distinction between the Human
Soul and the Body Are Demonstrated*

*To ⌈those most learned and most illustrious men,⌉ the Dean and Doctors of the Sacred Faculty of Theology of Paris*

Gentlemen:

My reason for offering you this work is so logical, and after you have learned its plan you will also, I am sure, have so logical a reason to take it under your protection, that I believe nothing will recommend it to you more than a brief statement of what I herein propose to do.

I have always thought that the two questions, of God and of the soul, were the principal questions among those that should be demonstrated by ⌈rational⌉ philosophy rather than theology. For although it may suffice us faithful ones to believe by faith that there is a God and that the human soul does not perish with the body, (2) certainly it does not seem possible ever to persuade those without faith to accept any religion, nor even perhaps any moral virtue, unless they can first be shown these two things by means of natural reason. And since in this life one frequently finds greater rewards offered for vice than for virtue, few persons would prefer the just to the useful if they were not restrained either by the fear of God or by the expectation of another life. It is absolutely true, both that we must believe that there is a God because it is so taught in the Holy Scriptures, and, on the other hand, that we must believe the Holy Scriptures because they come from God. The reason for this is that faith is a gift of God, and the very God that gives us the faith to believe other things can also give us the faith to believe that he [5] exists. Nevertheless, we could hardly offer this argument to those without faith, for they might suppose that we were committing the fallacy that logicians call circular reasoning.

And truly I have noticed that you, ⌈gentlemen,⌉ along with all other theologians, assure us not only that the existence of

God can be proved by natural reason, but also that we can infer from the Holy Scriptures that our knowledge of God is
much ⌜clearer ⌐and⌐ easier⌐ than our knowledge of various
created things, ⌜so clear⌐ in fact, ⌐so absolutely easy to attain,⌐
that those who do not possess it are blameworthy. This is evidenced in the words of the Book of the Wisdom of Solomon,
Chapter XIII, where it is said: "Howbeit they are not to be
excused; for if their understanding was so great that they
could discern the world and the creatures, why did they not
rather find out the Lord thereof?" And in the Epistle to the
Romans, Chapter I, where it is said that they are "without
excuse," and again in the same place in these words: "That
which may be known of God is manifest in them." It seems
that we are being told that all that can be known of God can
be demonstrated by reasons that we do not need to seek elsewhere than in ourselves, and that our minds alone are capable
of furnishing us. That is why I have believed that it would
not be inappropriate if I showed here how that can be done,
and by what means we can know God more easily and more
certainly than we know the things of the world.

And as for the soul, many have believed that it is not easy
to understand its nature, (3) and some have even dared to say
that human reasoning would convince us that it perishes with
the body, and that faith alone can teach us the contrary.
Nevertheless, as the Lateran Council, held under Leo X, Ses-
sion 8, condemns these persons, and expressly orders Christian
philosophers to refute their arguments and to employ all their
intellectual abilities to make the truth known, I have decided
to make the attempt in this work.

Moreover, the principal reason why many outside the Church
do not wish to believe that there is a God and that the human
soul is distinct from the body is that they claim that no one
has so far been able to demonstrate these two things. I do not
share their opinion; on the contrary, I hold that almost all of
the arguments brought to bear on these two questions by so
many illustrious men [6] are valid demonstrations when they
are properly understood, and that it is practically impossible

to invent new ones. So I believe that there is nothing more useful to be done in philosophy than ⌐critically and⌐ carefully to seek out, once and for all, the best ⌐and most reliable⌐ of such arguments, and to give them so clear and exact a presentation that it would thenceforward be evident to everyone that they are valid demonstrations. And finally, several persons have urged me to do this, since they knew that I have been practicing a certain method of solving all sorts of difficulties in the sciences—a method which really is not new, for nothing is older than the truth, but which they knew I was using rather successfully in other matters. I have therefore considered it my duty to see what I could achieve in this field. (4)

I have put in this treatise everything that I was able to discover about this subject. That is not to say that I have collected here all the various arguments which might be adduced as proofs in our subject, for I have never thought that that would be necessary unless no certain proof existed. I have only treated here of the most basic and principal ones in such a way that I can reasonably venture to maintain that they are very evident and very certain demonstrations. And I shall say further that they are such that I do not think there is any way in which the human mind can ever find better ones; for the importance of the subject, and the glory of God, to which all this relates, constrain me to speak somewhat more freely of myself here than I usually do. Nevertheless, whatever certainty and obviousness I find in my own arguments, I cannot convince myself that everyone will be able to understand them. There is a similar situation in geometry, where there are several proofs, left to us by Archimedes, Apollonius, Pappus, and several others, that are accepted by everyone as very certain and evident because they contain nothing but what, considered separately, is very easy to understand, and because there is no place where the consequences do not have an exact connection with and dependence upon their antecedents. Nevertheless, because these proofs are rather long and demand undivided attention, they are comprehended and understood by only a very few persons. In the same way, although I consider that the arguments I use here equal or even surpass in certainty and obviousness the [7] demonstrations of geometry, I nevertheless appreciate that they cannot be sufficiently well understood by many persons, partly because they also are somewhat lengthy and involved, but principally because they require a mind entirely free of all prejudice and one that can readily free itself from its attachment to the senses. And to tell the truth, there are not so many people in the world who are fitted for metaphysical speculations as there are those who are fitted for geometry. (5) There is this further difference, that in geometry everyone is persuaded that nothing should be written for which there is no certain proof. Therefore, those who are not well versed in the field are much more apt to make the mistake of accepting false demonstrations in order to make others believe that they understand them than they are to make the mistake of rejecting good ones. It is different in philosophy, where it is believed that there is nothing about which it is not possible to argue on either side. Thus few people engage in the search for truth, and many, who wish to acquire a reputation as clever thinkers, bend all their efforts to arrogant opposition to the most obvious truths.

That is why, ⌈gentlemen,⌉ since my arguments belong to philosophy, however strong they may be, I do not suppose that they will have any great effect unless you take them under your protection. But the esteem which everyone has for your Faculty is so great, and the name of the Sorbonne carries such authority, that not only is it more deferred to in matter of faith than any other group except the sacred councils, but even in human philosophy everyone agrees that it is impossible to find anywhere else so much reliability and knowledge, as well as prudence and integrity in the pronouncement of a judgment. Therefore, I do not doubt that if you will deign to give enough attention to this work so as to correct it—for, knowing not only my human fallibility but also my ignorance, I would not dare to affirm that it was free of error—and then to add to it whatever it lacks, to complete whatever is

imperfect, and yourselves either to take the trouble to give a
more adequate explanation of those points that need it or at
least to advise me of them so that I may work on them; and
finally, after the reasons by which I prove that there is a God
and that the human soul differs from the body have been
brought [8] to such a degree of clarity and obviousness, which
I am sure is possible, (6) that they should be considered very
exact demonstrations, if you then will deign to give them the
authority of your approbation and publicly testify to their
truth and certitude—I do not doubt, I say, that when this has
been done, all the errors and false opinions which have ever
been entertained on these two questions will soon be effaced
from the minds of men. For the expression of the truth will
cause all learned and wise men to subscribe to your judgment,
and your authority will cause the atheists, who are ordinarily
more arrogant than learned and judicious, to set aside their
spirit of contradiction, or perhaps themselves defend the arguments which they see being accepted as demonstrations by all
intelligent people, for fear of appearing not to understand
them. And finally, everyone else will easily accept the testi-
mony of so many witnesses, and there will no longer be anyone who dares to doubt the existence of God and the real and
true distinction between the human soul and the body.

It is for you, ⌐who now see the disorders which doubt of
these things produces,⌐ ⌐in your great wisdom⌐ to judge the
fruit which would grow out of such belief, once it were well
established; but it would not be fitting for me further to com-
mend the cause of God and religion to those who have always
been the firmest supporters ⌐of them ⌐and⌐ of the Catholic
Church⌐. (7) [9]

# PREFACE

I have already touched upon these two questions of God and of the human soul in the *Discourse on the Method of Rightly Conducting the Reason and Seeking Truth in the Sciences,* which I published in French in the year 1637. Then I was not concerned to give a complete discussion of the subjects, but only to treat of them in passing, in order to learn from the judgments of the readers in what way I should treat them afterward. For these questions have always seemed to me so important that I judged it appropriate to deal with them more than once. And the road I take to explain them is so little traveled and so far from the ordinary route that I did not think it would be useful to explain it in French in a discourse that might be read by anyone, for fear that those of feeble intellect would think it permissible for them to make the same attempt.

In the *Discourse on Method,* I requested everyone who found in my writings something worthy of criticism to do me the favor of informing me thereof. There were no noteworthy objections concerning these subjects except two, to which I shall here make a short reply before undertaking a more detailed presentation of them later.

The first objection is that it does not follow from the fact that the human mind, reflecting upon its own nature, (8) knows itself solely as a thinking being, that its nature or essence is only to think. The trouble is that this word "only" excludes all those other qualities that might perhaps also pertain to the nature of the mind.

To this objection I reply that it was not my intention at this point to exclude those qualities from the realm of objective reality, with which I was not then concerned, but only from the realm of my thought. My intention was to say that I knew nothing to pertain to my essence except that I was a being which thinks, that is, a being having in itself the faculty of thinking. Nevertheless, I shall show further on how it follows from the fact that I know nothing else which belongs to my essence that nothing else really does belong to it.

The second objection is that it does not follow from the fact that I have in my mind the idea of a thing more perfect than I am that this idea is more perfect than myself, much less that what is represented by this idea exists.

But I reply that in this word "idea" there is here an equivocation. For it can be taken materially, as an operation of my intellect, and in this sense it cannot be said to be more perfect than myself; or it can be taken objectively for the body which is represented by this operation, which, even though it is not supposed to exist outside of my understanding, can nevertheless be more perfect than myself in respect to its essence. In the rest of this treatise I shall show more fully how it follows from the mere fact that I have in my mind an idea of something more perfect than myself that this thing really exists.

In addition, I have seen two other rather long works on this subject which did not so much oppose my reasons as my conclusions, and this by arguments drawn from the commonplaces of the atheists. (9) But since arguments of this type cannot make any impression in the minds of those who fully understand my reasoning, and since the judgment of many persons is so weak and irrational that they much more often let themselves be convinced by the first opinions they hear on a subject, however false and unreasonable they may be, than by a refutation of their opinions which is valid and true but which is heard later, I do not wish to reply to the arguments here, for fear of being obliged first to report them.

I shall only say, in general, that the arguments which atheists use to combat the existence of God always depend either upon the assumption that God has human characteristics, or else upon the assumption that our own minds have so much ability and wisdom that we presume to delimit and comprehend what God can and should do. Thus all that atheists allege will give us no difficulty if only we remind ourselves that we should consider our minds to be finite and limited, and God to be an infinite and incomprehensible Being.

Now, having paid sufficient attention to the opinions of men, I undertake directly to treat of God and of the human mind, and at the same time to lay the foundations of first philosophy. I do this without expecting any praise for it from the vulgar, and without hoping that my book will be read by many. On the contrary, I would not recommend it to any except to those who would want to meditate seriously along with me, and who are capable of freeing the mind from attachment to the senses and clearing it entirely of all sorts of prejudices; and I know only too well that there are very few people of this sort. But as for those who do not care much about the order and connection of my arguments, and who amuse themselves by making clever remarks on the several parts, as (10) some will do—those persons, I say, will not profit much from reading this work. And although they may find opportunities for caviling in many places, they will hardly be able to make any objections which are important or which are worthy of reply.

And since I do not promise others to satisfy them wholly at the first attempt, and since I do not so far presume as to believe that I can foresee all that may entail difficulties for some people, I shall first present in these *Meditations* the same thoughts by which I think I have reached a certain and evident knowledge of the truth, in order to see whether I will be able to persuade others by means of the same reasons that have persuaded me. After that I shall reply to the objections which have been offered to me by people of insight and learning to whom I sent my *Meditations* to be examined before committing them to the press. These have been so numerous and so varied that I feel secure in believing that it would be difficult for anyone else to find an objection of consequence that has not already been treated.

That is why I beg my readers to suspend their judgment upon the *Meditations* until they have taken the trouble of reading all these objections and the replies that I have made to them. (11)

# SYNOPSIS OF THE SIX FOLLOWING
# MEDITATIONS

In the First Meditation, I offer the reasons why we can doubt all things in general, and particularly material objects, at least as long as we do not have other foundations for the sciences than those we have hitherto possessed. And although it is not immediately apparent that so general a doubt can be useful, it is in fact very much so, since it delivers us from all sorts of prejudices and makes available to us an easy method of accustoming our minds to become independent of the senses. Finally, it is useful in making it subsequently impossible to doubt those things which we discover to be true after we have taken doubt into consideration.

In the Second, the mind,[1] which in its intrinsic freedom supposes that everything which is open to the least doubt is nonexistent, recognizes that it is nevertheless absolutely impossible that it does not itself exist. This is also of the highest utility, since by this means the mind can easily distinguish between those qualities which belong to it—that is to say, to its intellectual nature—and those which belong to the body.

But because it might happen that some persons will expect me to offer at this point reasons to prove the immortality of the soul, I think it my duty to warn them now (13) that, since I have tried to write nothing in this treatise for which I did not have very exact demonstrations, I have found myself obliged to follow an order similar to that used by geometricians, which is to present first all those things on which the proposition one is seeking to prove depends, before reaching any conclusions about the proposition itself.

But the first and principal thing required in order to recognize the immortality of the soul [2] is to form the clearest possi-

1 [Latin: *mens;* French: *esprit.*]
2 [L. *anima;* F. *âme.*]

ble conception of it, [10] and one which is entirely distinct from all the conceptions one can have of the body, which has been done in this Second Meditation. It is necessary, in addition, to know that all things which we conceive clearly and distinctly are true in the manner in which we conceive them, and this cannot be proved before the Fourth Meditation. Furthermore, we must have a distinct conception of corporeal nature, which we acquire partly in the Second, and partly in the Fifth and Sixth Meditations. And finally, we must conclude from all this that things which we clearly and distinctly perceive to be diverse substances, as we conceive the mind and the body, are in fact substances which are really distinct from each other; which is what we conclude in the Sixth Meditation. This is confirmed again, in the same Meditation, by the fact that we cannot conceive any body except as divisible, while the mind or soul of man can only be conceived as indivisible. For in reality we cannot conceive of half of any soul, as we can of the smallest possible body, so that we recognize that their natures are not only different but even in some sense contrary. I have not treated this subject further in this treatise, partly because we have already discovered enough to show with sufficient clarity that the corruption of the body does not entail the death of the soul, and so to give men the hope of a second life after death; and partly because the premises from which the immortality of the soul may be concluded depend upon the explanation of the whole of physics. First, (14) we must know that all substances in general—that is to say, all those things which cannot exist without being created by God—are by nature incorruptible and can never cease to be, unless God himself, by denying them his usual support, reduces them to nothingness. And secondly, we must notice that body, taken in general, is a substance, and that it therefore will never perish. But the human body, however much it may differ from other bodies, is only a composite, produced by a certain configuration of members and by other similar accidents, whereas the human soul is not thus dependent upon any accidents, but is a pure substance. For even if all its accidents change—as, for example, if it conceives of certain things, wills others, and receives sense impressions of still others—nevertheless it still remains the same soul. But the human body becomes a different entity from the mere fact that the shape of some of its parts has been changed. From this it follows that the human body may very easily perish, but that the mind ⌈or soul of man, between which I find no distinction,⌉ is immortal by its very nature. [11]

In the Third Meditation, I have explained at sufficient length, it seems to me, the principal argument I use to prove the existence of God. Nevertheless, I did not want to use at that point any comparisons drawn from physical things, in order that the minds of the readers should be as far as possible withdrawn from the use of and commerce with the senses. There may, therefore, be many obscurities remaining, which I hope will be completely elucidated in my replies to the objections which have since been made to me. One of these obscurities is this: how can the idea of a supremely perfect Being, which we find in ourselves, contain so much objective reality, ⌈that is to say, how can it participate by representation in so many degrees of being and of perfection,⌉ that it must have come from a supremely perfect cause? This I have explained in these replies by means of a comparison with a very ⌈⌈ingenious and⌉ artificial machine, the idea of which occurs in the mind of some worker. For as the real cleverness of this idea must have some cause, I conclude it to be either the knowledge of this worker or that of some other from whom he has received this idea. In the same way (15) it is impossible that the idea of God, which is in us, does not have God himself as its cause.

In the Fourth, it is proved that all things which we ⌈conceive ⌈or⌉ perceive⌉ very clearly and very distinctly are wholly true. At the same time I explain the nature of error or falsity, which nature we ought to discover, as much to confirm the preceding truths as to understand better those that follow. Nevertheless, it should be noticed that I do not in any way treat here of sin—that is, of error committed in the pursuit of good and evil—but only of that which occurs in the judgment and discernment of the true and the false; and that I do not intend to speak of beliefs which belong to faith or to the conduct of life, but only of those which pertain to speculative truth and which can be known by the aid of the light of nature alone.

In the Fifth Meditation, besides the explanation of corporeal nature in general, the existence of God is again demonstrated by a new argument. There may also be some difficulties in this argument, but the solution will be found in the replies to the objections which have been made to me. In addition, I show how it is true that even the certainty of geometrical demonstrations themselves depends on the knowledge of God.

Finally, in the Sixth, I distinguish the action of the understanding from that of the imagination, and the marks of this distinction are described. Here I show that the ⸍mind ⸍or⸜ soul⸜ of man is really distinct from the body, and that nevertheless it is so tightly bound and united with it that it [12] forms with it what is almost a single entity. All the errors which arise from the senses are here exposed, together with the methods of avoiding them. And finally, I here bring out all the arguments from which we may conclude the existence of material things; not because I judge them very useful, in that they prove what (16) they do prove—namely, that there is a world, that men have bodies, and other similar things which have never been doubted by any man of good sense—but because, in considering these arguments more closely, we come to recognize that they are not as firm and as evident as those which lead us to the knowledge of God and of our soul, so that the latter are the most certain and most evident truths which can become known to the human mind. That is all that I had planned to prove in these *Meditations,* which leads me to omit here many other questions with which I have dealt incidentally in this treatise. (17) [13]

# FIRST MEDITATION

## CONCERNING THINGS THAT CAN BE DOUBTED

There is no novelty to me in the reflection that, from my earliest years, I have accepted many false opinions as true, and that what I have concluded from such badly assured premises could not but be highly doubtful and uncertain. From the time that I first recognized this fact, I have realized that if I wished to have any firm and constant knowledge in the sciences, I would have to undertake, once and for all, to set aside all the opinions which I had previously accepted among my beliefs and start again from the very beginning. But this enterprise appeared to me to be of very great magnitude, and so I waited until I had attained an age so mature that I could not hope for a later time when I would be more fitted to execute the project. Now, however, I have delayed so long that henceforward I should be ⌈afraid that I was⌉ committing a fault if, in continuing to deliberate, I expended time which should be devoted to action.

The present is opportune for my design; I have freed my mind of all kinds of cares; (18) ⌈I feel myself, fortunately, disturbed by no passions;⌉ and I have found a serene retreat in peaceful solitude. I will therefore make a serious and unimpeded effort to destroy generally all my former opinions. In order to do this, however, it will not be necessary to show that they are all false, a task [14] which I might never be able to complete; because, since reason already convinces me that I should abstain from the belief in things which are not entirely certain and indubitable no less carefully than from the belief in those which appear to me to be manifestly false, it will be enough to make me reject them all if I can find in each some ground for doubt. And for that it will not be necessary for me to examine each one in particular, which would be an infinite labor; but since the destruction of the foundation necessarily involves the collapse of all the rest of the edifice, I shall first attack the principles upon which all my former opinions were founded.

Everything which I have thus far accepted as entirely true ⌈and assured⌉ has been acquired from the senses or by means of the senses. But I have learned by experience that these senses sometimes mislead me, and it is prudent never to trust wholly those things which have once deceived us.

But it is possible that, even though the senses occasionally deceive us about things which are barely perceptible and very far away, there are many other things which we cannot reasonably doubt, even though we know them through the senses —as, for example, that I am here, seated by the fire, wearing a ⌐winter⌐ dressing gown, holding this paper in my hands, and other things of this nature. And how could I deny that these hands and this body are mine, unless I am to compare myself with certain lunatics (19) whose brain is so troubled and befogged by the black vapors of the bile that they continually affirm that they are kings while they are paupers, that they are clothed in ⌈gold and⌉ purple while they are naked; or imagine ⌐that their head is made of clay, or⌐ that they are gourds, or that their body is glass? ⌈But this is ridiculous;⌉ such men are fools, and I would be no less insane than they if I followed their example.

Nevertheless, I must remember that I am a man, and that consequently I am accustomed to sleep and in my dreams to imagine the same things that lunatics imagine when awake, or sometimes things which are even less plausible. How many times has it occurred that ⌐the quiet of⌐ the night made me dream ⌐of my usual habits:⌐ that I was here, clothed ⌐in a dressing gown⌐, and sitting by the fire, although I was in fact lying undressed in bed! It seems apparent to me now, that I am not looking at this paper with my eyes closed, that this head that I shake is not drugged with sleep, that it is with design and deliberate intent that I stretch out this hand and perceive it. What happens in sleep seems not at all as clear and as distinct as all this. [15] But I am speaking as though I never recall having been misled, while asleep, by similar illusions! When I consider these matters carefully, I realize so clearly that there are no conclusive indications by which waking life can be distinguished from sleep that I am quite astonished, and my bewilderment is such that it is almost able to convince me that I am sleeping.

So let us suppose now that we are asleep and that all these details, such as opening the eyes, shaking the head, extending the hands, and similar things, are merely illusions; and let us think that perhaps our hands and our whole body are not such as we see them. Nevertheless, we must at least admit that these things which appear to us in sleep are like ⌐painted⌐ scenes ⌐and portraits⌐ which can only be formed in imitation of something ⌐real and⌐ true, and so, at the very least, these types of things—namely, eyes, head, hands, and the whole body—are not imaginary entities, but real and existent. For in truth painters, even when (20) they use the greatest ingenuity in attempting to portray sirens and satyrs in ⌐bizarre and⌐ extraordinary ways, nevertheless cannot give them wholly new shapes and natures, but only invent some particular mixture composed of parts of various animals; or even if perhaps ⌐their imagination is sufficiently extravagant that⌐ they invent something so new that nothing like it has ever been seen, and so their work represents something purely imaginary and ⌐absolutely⌐ false, certainly at the very least the colors of which they are composed must be real.

And for the same reason, even if these types of things—namely, ⌐a body,⌐ eyes, head, hands, and other similar things—could be imaginary, nevertheless, we are bound to confess that there are some other still more simple and universal concepts which are true ⌐and existent⌐, from the mixture of which, neither more nor less than in the case of the mixture of real colors, all these images of things are formed in our minds, whether they are true ⌐and real⌐ or imaginary ⌐and fantastic⌐.

Of this class of entities is corporeal nature in general and its extension, including the shape of extended things, their quantity, or size and number, and also the place where they are, the time that measures their duration, and so forth. [16] That is why we will perhaps not be reasoning badly if we conclude that physics, astronomy, medicine, and all the other sciences which follow from the consideration of composite entities are very dubious [and uncertain]; whereas arithmetic, geometry, and the other sciences of this nature, which treat only of very simple and general things without concerning themselves as to whether they occur in nature or not, contain some element of certainty and sureness. For whether I am awake or whether I am asleep, two and three together will always make the number five, and the square will never have more than four sides; and it does not seem possible that truths [so clear and] so apparent can ever be suspected of any falsity [or uncertainty]. (21)

Nevertheless, I have long held the belief that there is a God who can do anything, by whom I have been created and made what I am. But how can I be sure but that he has brought it to pass that there is no earth, no sky, no extended bodies, no shape, no size, no place, and that nevertheless I have the impressions of all these things [and cannot imagine that things might be other than] as I now see them? And furthermore, just as I sometimes judge that others are mistaken about those things which they think they know best, how can I be sure but that [God has brought it about that] I am always mistaken when I add two and three or count the sides of a square, or when I judge of something else even easier, if I can imagine anything easier than that? But perhaps God did not wish me to be deceived in that fashion, since he is said to be supremely good. But if it was repugnant to his goodness to have made me so that I was always mistaken, it would seem also to be inconsistent for him to permit me to be sometimes mistaken, and nevertheless I cannot doubt that he does permit it.

At this point there will perhaps be some persons who would prefer to deny the existence of so powerful a God, rather than to believe that everything else is uncertain. Let us not oppose them for the moment, and let us concede ⌜according to their point of view⌝ that everything which I have stated here about God is fictitious. Then in whatever way they suppose that I have reached the state of being that I now have, whether they attribute it to some destiny or fate or refer it to chance, or whether they wish to explain it as the result of a continual interplay of events ⟨or in any other manner⟩; nevertheless, since to err and be mistaken [17] is a kind of imperfection, to whatever degree less powerful they consider the author to whom they attribute my origin, in that degree it will be more probable that I am so imperfect that I am always mistaken. To this reasoning, certainly, I have nothing to reply; and I am at last constrained to admit that there is nothing in what I formerly believed to be true which I cannot somehow doubt, and this not for lack of thought and attention, but for weighty and well-considered reasons. Thus I find that, in the future, I should ⌜withhold and suspend my judgment about these matters, and⌝ guard myself no less carefully from believing them than I should from believing what is manifestly false (22) if I wish to find any certain and assured knowledge ⌜in the sciences⌝.

It is not enough to have made these observations; it is also necessary that I should take care to bear them in mind. For these customary and long-standing beliefs will frequently recur in my thoughts, my long and familiar acquaintance with them giving them the right to occupy my mind against my will ⌜and almost to make themselves masters of my beliefs⌝. I will never free myself of the habit of deferring to them and having faith in them as long as I consider that they are what they really are—that is, somewhat doubtful, as I have just shown, even if highly probable—so that there is much more reason to believe than to deny them. That is why I think that I would not do badly if I deliberately took the opposite position and deceived myself in pretending for some time that all these opinions are entirely false and imaginary, until at last I will have so balanced my former and my new prejudices that they cannot incline my mind more to one side than the other, and my judgment will not be ⌈mastered and⌉ turned by bad habits from the ⌠correct perception of things ⌈and the⌠ straight road leading to the knowledge of the truth⌉. For I feel sure that I cannot overdo this distrust, since it is not now a question of acting, but only of ⌈meditating and⌉ learning.

I will therefore suppose that, not ⌈a true⌉ God, ⌠who is very good and⌠ who is the supreme source of truth, but a certain evil spirit, not less clever and deceitful than powerful, has bent all his efforts to deceiving me. I will suppose that the sky, the air, the earth, colors, shapes, sounds, and all other objective things ⌈that we see⌉ are nothing but illusions and dreams that he [18] has used to trick my credulity. I will consider (23) myself as having no hands, no eyes, no flesh, no blood, nor any senses, yet falsely believing that I have all these things. I will remain resolutely attached to this hypothesis; and if I cannot attain the knowledge of any truth by this method, at any rate ⌈it is in my power to suspend my judgment. That is why⌉ I shall take great care not to accept any falsity among my beliefs and shall prepare my mind so well for all the ruses of this great deceiver that, however powerful and artful he may be, he will never be able to mislead me in anything.

But this undertaking is arduous, and a certain laziness leads me insensibly into the normal paths of ordinary life. I am like a slave who, enjoying an imaginary liberty during sleep, begins to suspect that his liberty is only a dream; he fears to wake up and conspires with his pleasant illusions to retain them longer. So insensibly to myself I fall into my former opinions; and I am slow to wake up from this slumber for fear that the labors of waking life which will have to follow the tranquillity of this sleep, instead of leading me into the daylight of the knowledge of the truth, will be insufficient to dispel the darkness of all the difficulties which have just been raised.

# SECOND MEDITATION

## OF THE NATURE OF THE HUMAN MIND, AND THAT IT IS MORE EASILY KNOWN THAN THE BODY

Yesterday's Meditation has filled my mind with so many doubts that it is no longer in my power to forget them. Nor do I yet see how I will be able to resolve them; I feel as though (24) I were suddenly thrown into deep water, being so disconcerted that I can neither plant my feet on the bottom nor swim on the surface. I shall nevertheless make every effort to conform precisely to the plan commenced yesterday and put aside every belief in which I could imagine the least doubt, just as though I knew that it was absolutely [19] false. And I shall continue in this manner until I have found something certain, or at least, if I can do nothing else, until I have learned with certainty that there is nothing certain in this world. Archimedes, to move the earth from its orbit and place it in a new position, demanded nothing more than a fixed and immovable fulcrum; in a similar manner I shall have the right to entertain high hopes if I am fortunate enough to find a single truth which is certain and indubitable.

I suppose, accordingly, that everything that I see is false; I convince myself that nothing has ever existed of all that my deceitful memory recalls to me. I think that I have no senses; and I believe that body, shape, extension, motion, and location are merely inventions of my mind. What then could still be thought true? Perhaps nothing else, unless it is that there is nothing certain in the world.

But how do I know that there is not some entity, of a different nature from what I have just judged uncertain, of which there cannot be the least doubt? Is there not some God or some other power who gives me these thoughts? But I need not think this to be true, for possibly I am able to produce them myself. Then, at the very least, am I not an entity myself? But I have already denied that I had any senses or any body. However, at this point I hesitate, for what (25) follows from that? Am I so dependent upon the body and the senses that I could not exist without them? I have just convinced myself that nothing whatsoever existed in the world, that there was no sky, no earth, no minds, and no bodies; have I not thereby convinced myself that I did not exist? Not at all; without doubt I existed if I was convinced ⌈or even if I thought anything⌉. Even though there may be a deceiver of some sort, very powerful and very tricky, who bends all his efforts to keep me perpetually deceived, there can be no slightest doubt that I exist, since he deceives me; and let him deceive me as much as he will, he can never make me be nothing as long as I think that I am something. Thus, after having thought well on this matter, and after examining all things with care, I must finally conclude and maintain that this proposition: *I am, I exist,* is necessarily true every time that I pronounce it or conceive it in my mind.

But I do not yet know sufficiently clearly what I am, I who am sure that I exist. So I must henceforth take very great care that I do not incautiously mistake [20] some other thing for myself, and so make an error even in that knowledge which I maintain to be more certain and more evident than all other knowledge ⌈that I previously had⌉. That is why I shall now consider once more what I thought myself to be before I began these last deliberations. Of my former opinions I shall reject all that are rendered even slightly doubtful by the arguments that I have just now offered, so that there will remain just that part alone which is entirely certain and indubitable.

What then have I previously believed myself to be? Clearly, I believed that I was a man. But what is a man? Shall I say a rational animal? Certainly not, for I would have to determine what an "animal" is and what is meant by "rational"; and so, from a single question, I would find myself gradually enmeshed in an infinity of others more difficult ⌈and more inconvenient⌉, and I would not care to waste the little time and

leisure remaining to me in disentangling such difficulties. I
shall rather pause here to consider the ideas which previously
arose naturally and of themselves (26) in my mind whenever I
considered what I was. I thought of myself first as having a
face, hands, arms, and all this mechanism composed of ⌈bone
and flesh ⌐and⌐ members⌐, just as it appears in a corpse, and
which I designated by the name of "body." In addition, I
thought of the fact that I consumed nourishment, that I
walked, that I perceived and thought, and I ascribed all these
actions to the soul. But either I did not stop to consider what
this soul was or else, if I did, I imagined that it was something
very rarefied and subtle, such as a wind, a flame, or a very
much expanded air which ⌈penetrated into and⌐ was infused
thoughout my grosser components. As for what body was, I
did not realize that there could be any doubt about it, for I
thought that I recognized its nature very distinctly. If I had
wished to explain it according to the notions that I then entertained, I would have described it somewhat in this way: By
"body" I understand all that can be bounded by some figure:
that can be located in some place and occupy space in such a
way that every other body is excluded from it; that can be
perceived by touch or sight or hearing or taste or smell; that
can be moved in various ways, not by itself but by some other
object by which it is touched ⌈and from which it receives an
impulse⌐. For to possess the power to move itself, and also to
feel or to think, I did not believe at all that these are attributes of corporeal nature; on the contrary, rather, I was astonished [21] to see a few bodies possessing such abilities.

   But I, what am I, on the basis of the present hypothesis that
there is a certain spirit who is extremely powerful and, if I
may dare to say so, malicious ⌈and tricky⌐, and who uses all his
abilities and efforts in order to deceive me? Can I be sure that
I possess the smallest fraction of all those characteristics which
I have just now said belonged to the nature of body? (27) I
pause to consider this attentively. I pass and repass in review
in my mind each one of all these things—it is not necessary to
pause to take the time to list them—and I do not find any one

of them which I can pronounce to be part of me. Let us move
on to the attributes of the soul and see if any of these are in me.
Is it characteristic of me to consume nourishment and to walk?
But if it is true that I do not have a body, these also are nothing
but figments of the imagination. To perceive?[1] But once more,
I cannot perceive without the body, except in the sense that I
have thought I perceived various things during sleep, which I
recognized upon waking not to have been really perceived. To
think?[2] Here I find the answer. Thought is an attribute that
belongs to me; it alone is inseparable from my nature.

exists as long as he thinks

I am, I exist—that is certain; but for how long do I exist?
For as long as I think; for it might perhaps happen, if I to-
tally ceased thinking, that I would at the same time completely cease to be. I am now admitting nothing except what
is necessarily true. I am therefore, to speak precisely, only a
thinking being, that is to say, a mind, an understanding,[3] or a
reasoning being, which are terms whose meaning was previously unknown to me.

I am something real and really existing, but what thing am
I? I have already given the answer: a thing which thinks. And
what more? I will stimulate my imagination ⌈to see if I am
not something else beyond this⌉. I am not this assemblage of
members which is called a human body; I am not a rarefied
and penetrating air spread throughout all these members; I
am not a wind, ⌈a flame,⌉ a breath, a vapor, or anything at all
that I can imagine and picture to myself—since I have supposed that all that was nothing, and since, without abandon-
ing this supposition, I find that I do not cease to be certain
that I am something.

But perhaps it is true that those same things which I suppose not to exist because I do not know them are really no
different from the self which I do know. As to that I cannot
decide; I am not discussing that question at the moment, since
I can pass judgment only upon those things which are known
to me: I know that I exist and I am seeking to discover what

1 [L. *sentire;* F. *sentir.*]
2 [L. *cogitare;* F. *penser.*]
3 [L. *intellectus;* F. *entendement.*]

I am, that "I" that I know to be. Now it is very [22] certain that this notion ⌈and knowledge of my being⌉, thus precisely understood, does not depend on things whose existence (28) is not yet known to me; and consequently ⌈and even more certainly⌉, it does not depend on any of those things that I ⌈⌈can⌉⌉ picture in my imagination. And even these terms, "picture" and "imagine," warn me of my error. For I would be imagining falsely indeed were I to picture myself as something; since to imagine is nothing else than to contemplate the shape or image of a bodily entity, and I already know both that I certainly exist and that it is altogether possible that all these images, and everything in general which is involved in the nature of body, are only dreams ⌈and illusions⌉. From this I see clearly that there was no more sense in saying that I would stimulate my imagination to learn more distinctly what I am than if I should say: I am now awake, and I see something real and true; but because I do not yet perceive it sufficiently clearly, I will go to sleep on purpose, in order that my dreams will show it to me with more truth and evidence. And thus I know manifestly that nothing of all that I can understand by means of the imagination is pertinent to the knowledge which I have of myself, and that I must remember this and prevent my mind from thinking in this fashion, in order that it may clearly perceive its own nature.

But what then am I? A thinking being.[4] What is a thinking being? It is a being which doubts, which understands, ⌈which conceives,⌉ which affirms, which denies, which wills, which rejects, which imagines also, and which perceives. It is certainly not a trivial matter if all these things belong to my nature. But why should they not belong to it? Am I not that same person who now doubts almost everything, who nevertheless understands ⌈and conceives⌉ certain things, who ⌈is sure of and⌉ affirms the truth of this one thing alone, who denies all the others, who wills and desires to know more about them, who rejects error, who imagines many things, sometimes even against my will, and who also perceives many things, as

4 [L. *res cogitans;* F. *une chose qui pense.*]

through the medium of ⸝the senses ⌐or⸌ the organs of the body⌐? Is there anything in all that which is not just as true as it is certain that I am and that I exist, even though I were always asleep (29) and though the one who created me directed all his efforts to deluding me? And is there any one of these attributes which can be distinguished from my thinking or which can be said to be separable from my nature? For it is so obvious that it is I who doubt, understand, and desire, that nothing could be added to make it more evident. And I am also certainly the same one who imagines; [23] for once more, even though it could happen that the things I imagine are not true, nevertheless this power of imagining cannot fail to be real, and it is part of my thinking. Finally I am the same being which perceives—that is, which observes certain objects as though by means of the sense organs, because I do really see light, hear noises, feel heat. Will it be said that these appearances are false and that I am sleeping? ⌐Let it be so; yet at the very least⌐ it is certain that it seems to me that I see light, hear noises, and feel heat. This much cannot be false, and it is this, properly considered, which in my nature is called perceiving, and that, again speaking precisely, is nothing else but thinking.

As a result of these considerations, I begin to recognize what I am ⸝somewhat better ⌐and⸌ with a little more clarity and distinctness⌐ than heretofore. But nevertheless ⸝it still seems to me, and⸌ I cannot keep myself from believing that corporeal things, images of which are formed by thought and which the senses themselves examine, are ⸝much⸌ more distinctly known than that indescribable part of myself which cannot be pictured by the imagination. Yet it would truly be very strange to say that I know and comprehend more distinctly things whose existence seems doubtful to me, that are unknown to me and do not belong to me, than those of whose truth I am persuaded, which are known to me, and which belong to my real nature ⸝—to say, in a word, that I know them better than myself⸌. But I see well what is the trouble: my mind ⸝is a vagabond who⸌ likes to wander and is not yet able to stay

within the strict bounds of truth. Therefore, let us ⌐give it
the rein once more ⌐and⌐ allow it every kind of liberty,
(30) ⌐permitting it to consider the objects which appear to be
external,⌐⌐ so that when a little later we come to restrain it
⌐gently and⌐ at the right time ⌐and force it to the consideration of its own nature and of the things that it finds in itself⌐,
it will more readily permit itself to be ruled and guided.

Let us now consider the ⌐commonest⌐ things, which are
commonly believed to be the most distinctly known ⌐⌐and the
easiest of all to know⌐⌐, namely, the bodies which we touch
and see. I do not intend to speak of bodies in general, for general notions are usually somewhat more confused; let us
rather consider one body in particular. Let us take, for example, this bit of wax which has just been taken from the
hive. It has not yet completely lost the sweetness of the honey
it contained; it still retains something of the odor of the
flowers from which it was collected; its color, shape, and size
are apparent; it is hard and cold; it can easily be touched;
and, if you knock on it, it will give out some sound. Thus
everything which can make a body distinctly known are found
in this example.

But now while I am talking I bring it close to the fire.
What remains of the taste evaporates; the odor vanishes; its
color changes; its shape is lost; its size increases; it becomes
liquid; it grows hot; one can hardly touch it; and although it
is knocked upon, it [24] will give out no sound. Does the same
wax remain after this change? We must admit that it does; no
one denies it ⌐, no one judges otherwise⌐. What is it then in
this bit of wax that we recognize with so much distinctness?
Certainly it cannot be anything that I observed by means of
the senses, since everything in the field of taste, smell, sight,
touch, and hearing are changed, and since the same wax
nevertheless remains.

The truth of the matter perhaps, as I now suspect, is that
this wax was neither that sweetness of honey, nor that ⌐pleas-
ant⌐ odor of flowers, nor that whiteness, nor that shape, nor
that sound, but only a body which a little while ago appeared

to my senses under these forms and which now makes itself
felt under others. But what is it, to speak precisely, that I
imagine ⌐when I conceive it⌐ in this fashion? Let us consider
it attentively (31) and, rejecting everything that does not belong to the wax, see what remains. Certainly nothing is left
but something extended, flexible, and movable. But what is
meant by flexible and movable? Does it consist in my pic-
turing that this wax, being round, is capable of becoming
square and of passing from the square into a triangular shape?
Certainly not; ⌐it is not that,⌐ since I conceive it capable of
undergoing an infinity of similar changes, and I could not
compass this infinity in my imagination. Consequently this
conception that I have of the wax is not achieved by the faculty of imagination.

Now what is this extension? Is it not also unknown? For it
becomes greater in the melting wax, still greater when it is
completely melted, and much greater again when the heat increases still more. And I would not conceive ⌐clearly and⌐
truthfully what wax was if I did not think that even this bit
of wax is capable of receiving more variations in extension
than I have ever imagined. We must therefore agree that I
cannot even conceive what this bit of wax is by means of the
imagination, and that there is nothing but my understanding [5] alone which does conceive it. I say this bit of wax in
particular, for as to wax in general, it is still more evident.
But what is this bit of wax which cannot be comprehended
except by ⌐the understanding, or by⌐ the mind? Certainly it is
the same as the one that I see, that I touch, that I imagine;
and finally it is the same as I always believed it to be from the
beginning. But what is here important to notice is that perception [6] ⌐,or the action by which we perceive,⌐ is not a vision,
a touch, nor an imagination, and has never been that, even
though it formerly appeared so; [25] but is solely an inspec-
tion by the mind, which can be imperfect and confused as it

5 [L. *mens;* F. *entendement.*]
6 [L. *perceptio;* F. *perception.*]

was formerly, or clear and distinct as it is at present, as I attend more or less to the things ⌐which are in it and⌐ of which it is composed.

Now I am truly astonished when I consider ⌐how weak my mind is and⌐ how apt I am to fall into error. For even though I consider all this in my mind without speaking, (32) still words impede me, and I am nearly deceived by the terms of ordinary language. For we say that we see the same wax if it is present, and not that we judge that it is the same from the fact that it has the same color or shape. Thus I might be tempted to conclude that one knows the wax by means of eyesight, and not uniquely by the perception of the mind. So I may by chance look out of a window and notice some men passing in the street, at the sight of whom I do not fail to say that I see men, just as I say that I see wax; and nevertheless what do I see from this window except hats and cloaks which might cover ⌐ghosts, or⌐ automata ⌐which move only by springs⌐? But I judge that they are men, and thus I comprehend, solely by the faculty of judgment which resides in my mind, that which I believed I saw with my eyes.

A person who attempts to improve his understanding beyond the ordinary ought to be ashamed to go out of his way to criticize the forms of speech used by ordinary men. I prefer to pass over this matter and to consider whether I understood what wax was more evidently and more perfectly when I first noticed it and when I thought I knew it by means of the external senses, or at the very least by common sense, as it is called, or the imaginative faculty; or whether I conceive it better at present, after having more carefully examined what it is and how it can be known. Certainly it would be ridiculous to doubt the superiority of the latter method of knowing. For what was there in that first perception which was distinct ⌐and evident⌐? What was there which might not occur similarly to the senses of the lowest of the animals? But when I distinguished the real wax from its superficial appearances, and when, just as though I had removed its garments, I consider it all naked, it is certain that although there might still be some error in my judgment, I could not conceive it in this fashion without a human mind. (33)

And now what shall I say of the mind, that is to say, of myself? For so far I do not admit in myself anything other than the mind. Can it be that I, who seem to perceive this bit of wax [26] so ⌈clearly and⌉ distinctly, do not know my own self, not only with much more truth and certainty, but also much more distinctly and evidently? For if I judge that the wax exists because I see it, certainly it follows much more evidently that I exist myself because I see it. For it might happen that what I see is not really wax; it might also happen that I do not even possess eyes to see anything; but it could not happen that, when I see, or what amounts to the same thing, when I think I see, I who think am not something. For a similar reason, if I judge that the wax exists because I touch it, the same conclusion follows once more, namely, that I am. And if I hold to this judgment because my imagination, or whatever other entity it might be, persuades me of it, I will still reach the same conclusion. And what I have said here about the wax can be applied to all other things which are external to me.

Furthermore, if the idea or knowledge of the wax seems clearer and more distinct to me after I have investigated it, not only by sight or touch, but also in many other ways, with how much more ⌈evidence,⌉ distinctness ⌈and clarity⌉ must it be admitted that I now know myself; since all the reasons which help me to know and conceive the nature of the wax, or of any other body whatsoever, serve much better to show the nature of my mind! And we also find so many other things in the mind itself which can contribute to the clarification of its nature, that those which depend on the body, such as the ones I have just mentioned, hardly deserve to be taken into account.

And at last here I am, having insensibly returned to where (34) I wished to be; for since it is at present manifest to me that even bodies are not properly known by the senses nor by the faculty of imagination, but by the understanding alone; and since they are not known in so far as they are seen or touched, but only in so far as they are understood by thinking, I see clearly that there is nothing easier for me to understand than my mind. But since it is almost impossible to rid oneself so soon of an opinion of long standing, it would be wise to stop a while at this point, in order that, by the length of my meditation, I may impress this new knowledge more deeply upon my memory. [27]

# THIRD MEDITATION

## OF GOD: THAT HE EXISTS

Now I shall close my eyes, I shall stop my ears, I shall disregard my senses, I shall even efface from my mind all the images of corporeal things; or at least, since that can hardly be done, I shall consider them vain and false. By thus dealing only with myself and considering what is included in me, I shall try to make myself, little by little, better known and more familiar to myself.

I am a thing which thinks, that is to say, which doubts, which affirms, which denies, which knows a few things, which is ignorant of many, ⌐which loves, which hates,⌐ which wills, which rejects, which imagines also, and which senses. For as I have previously remarked, although the things which I sense and which I imagine are perhaps nothing at all apart from me ⌐and in themselves⌐, I am nevertheless sure that those modes of thought which I call sensations and imaginations, (35) only just as far as they are modes of thought, reside and are found with certainty in myself.

And in this short statement I think I have reported all that I truly know, or at least all that I have so far noticed that I know. Now, ⌐in order to try to extend my knowledge further,⌐1 I shall ⌐be circumspect and⌐ consider with care if I cannot still discover in myself some other bits of knowledge which I have not yet observed. I am sure that I am a thinking being; but do I not then know what is required to make me sure of something? Certainly, in this first conclusion, there is nothing else which assures me of its truth but the clear and distinct perception of what I affirm. But this would really not be sufficient to assure me that what I affirm is true if it could ever happen that something which I conceived just as clearly and distinctly should prove false. And therefore it seems to me that I can already establish as a general principle that everything which we conceive very clearly and very distinctly is wholly true.

I have, however, previously accepted and admitted several things as very certain and very obvious which I have nevertheless subsequently recognized to be doubtful and uncertain. What, then, were those things? They were the earth, the sky, the stars, and all the other things I perceived through the medium of my senses. But [28] what did I conceive [1] clearly ⌐and distinctly⌐ in them? Nothing, certainly, unless that the ideas or thoughts of those things were present to my mind. And even now I do not deny the occurrence of these ideas in me. But there was still another thing of which I was sure and which, because of my habit of believing it, I thought I perceived very clearly, although in truth I did not perceive it at all—namely, that there were things outside of myself from which these ideas came and to which they were completely similar. That was the point in which, perhaps, I was mistaken; or at any rate, even if my judgment was in accord with the truth, it was no knowledge of mine which produced the truth of my judgment.

But when I considered something very simple and very easy concerning arithmetic and geometry, (36) as, for example, that two and three joined together produce the number five, and other similar things, did I not conceive them at least sufficiently clearly to guarantee that they were true? Certainly, if

---

[1] [L. percipio; F. concevoir.]

I have since judged that these things might be doubted, it was
for no other reason than that it occurred to me that some God
might perhaps have given me such a nature that I would be
mistaken even about those things that seemed most obvious to
me. Every time that this idea of the supreme power of a God,
as previously conceived, occurs to me, I am constrained to admit that it is easy for him, if he wishes it, to bring it about
that I am wrong even in those matters which I believe I perceive ⟨with the mind's eye⟩ with the greatest ⟨possible⟩ obviousness. And on the other hand, every time I turn to the
things I think I conceive very clearly, I am so convinced by
them that I am spontaneously led to proclaim: "Let him deceive me who can; he will never be able to bring it about that
I am nothing while I think I am something, or, it being true
that I now am, that it will some day be true that I have never
been, or that two and three joined together make more or less
than five, or similar things ⟨in which I recognize a manifest
contradiction ⌈and⌉ which I see clearly could not be otherwise
than as I conceive them⌉."

And certainly, since I have no reason to believe that there
is a God who is a deceiver, and since I have not yet even considered those reasons that prove that there is a God, the argument for doubting which depends only on this opinion is very
tenuous and, so to speak, metaphysical. But in order to remove it altogether I must examine whether there is a God as
soon as an opportunity occurs, and if I find that there is one I
must also investigate whether he can be [29] a deceiver; for as
long as this is unknown, I do not see that I can ever be certain of anything. And now, ⌈in order that I shall have an opportunity to examine this question without interrupting the
order of thought which I have proposed for myself, which is
to pass by degrees from the notions which I discover to be
most basic in my mind to those that I can discover afterward,⌉
⟨good order seems to demand that⟩ I should first classify all
(37) my thoughts into certain types and consider in which of
these types there is, properly, truth or error.

Among my thoughts some are like images of objects, and it

is to these alone that the name of "idea" properly applies, as when I picture to myself a man, or a chimera, or the sky, or an angel, or God ⌐himself⌐. Then there are others with different forms, as when I wish, or fear, or affirm, or deny. In these cases I do conceive something as the object of the action of my mind, but I also add something else by this action to the idea which I have of the entity; and of this type of thought, some are called volitions or emotions, and others judgments.

Now as far as ideas are concerned, if we consider them only in themselves and do not relate them to something else, they cannot, properly speaking, be false; for whether I imagine a sage or a satyr, it is no less true that I imagine the one than the other. Similarly, we must not fear to encounter falsity in the emotions or volitions; for even though I may desire bad things, or even things which never existed, nevertheless it is no less true on that account that I desire them. So there is nothing left but judgments alone, in which I must take very great care not to make a mistake. But the principal and most common error which can be encountered here consists in judging that the ideas which are in myself are similar to, or conformable to, things outside of myself; for certainly, if I considered the ideas only as certain modes ⌐or aspects⌐ of my thought, without intending them to refer to some other exterior object, they could hardly offer me a chance of making a mistake.

Among these ideas, some seem to be born with me, others to ⌐be alien to me and to⌐ come from without, (38) and the rest to be made ⌐and invented⌐ by myself. For I have the ability to conceive what is generally called a thing, or a truth, or a thought; and it seems to me that I do not conceive this from anything but my own nature. But if I now hear some noise, if I [30] see the sun, if I feel heat, I have hitherto judged that these feelings proceeded from some things which exist outside of myself; and finally, it seems to me that sirens, hippogriffs, and ⌐all other⌐ similar chimeras are fictions and inventions of my mind. Perhaps I might persuade myself that all these ideas are ⌐of the type of those I call⌐ alien ⌐and which

come from withoutl, or perhaps they are all innate, or perhaps they might all be invented; for I have not yet clearly discovered their true origin. And what I must principally do at
this point is to consider, concerning those which seem to me
to come from objects outside of me, what evidence obliges me
to believe that they resemble those objects.

The first of these reasons is that it seems to me that nature
teaches me so, and the second that I have direct experience
that these ideas are not dependent upon my will /nor upon
myself\. For often they come to me despite my wishes; just as
now, whether I wish it or not, I feel heat, and for that reason
I conclude that this sensation, or rather this idea, of heat is
produced in me by something different from myself, namely,
by the heat of the fire near which I am sitting. And I see nothing which appears more reasonable to me than to judge that
this alien entity sends to me and imposes upon me its likeness
rather than anything else.

Now I must see whether these reasons are sufficiently strong
and convincing. When I say that it seems to me that nature
teaches me so, I understand by this word "nature" only a certain inclination which leads me to believe it, and not the light
of nature which makes me know that it is true. But these two
expressions are very different from each other; for I could not
doubt in any way what the light of nature made me see to be
true, just as it made me see, a little while ago, that from the
fact that I doubted I could conclude that I existed. And /there
is no way in which this could be doubted, because\ I have no
other faculty or power to distinguish the true from the false
which could teach me that what this light of nature shows me
as true is not so, and in which I could trust as much as in the
light of nature itself. (39) But as for inclinations, which also
seem to me to be natural, I have often noticed, when it was a
question of choosing between virtues and vices, that they led
me to the bad no less than to the good; and for this reason I
have not been inclined to follow them even in what concerns
the true and the false. [31]

As for the other reason, which is that these ideas must come from elsewhere, since they do not depend upon my will, I do not find this convincing either. For just as the inclinations which we are now considering occur in me, despite the fact that they are not always in accord with my will, so perhaps there is in me some faculty or power adequate to produce these ideas without the aid of any external objects, even though it is not yet known to me; just as it has so far always seemed to me that when I sleep, these ideas are formed in me without the aid of the objects which they represent. And finally, even if I should agree that the ideas are caused by these objects, it does not necessarily follow that they should be similar to them. On the contrary, I have often observed in many instances that there was a great difference between the object and its idea. Thus, for example, I find in myself two completely different ideas of the sun: the one has its origin in the senses, and must be placed in the class of those that, as I said before, came from without, according to which it seems to me extremely small; the other is derived from astronomical considerations—that is, from certain innate ideas—or at least is formed by myself in whatever way it may be, according to which it seems to me many times greater than the whole earth. Certainly, these two ideas of the sun cannot both be similar to the same sun ⟨existing outside of me⟩, and reason makes me believe that the one which comes directly from its appearance is that which least resembles it.

All this makes me recognize sufficiently well that up to now it has not been by (40) a valid and considered judgment, but only by a blind ⌈and rash⌉ impulse, that I have believed that there were things outside of myself and different from my own being which, through the organs of my senses or by whatever other method it might be, sent into me their ideas or images ⌈and impressed upon me their resemblances⌉.

But there is still another path by which to seek if, among the things of which I possess ideas, there are some which exist outside of myself. If these ideas are considered only in so far as they are particular modes of thought, I do not recognize any ⌈difference or⌉ inequality among them, and all of them

appear to arise from myself in the same fashion. But considering them as images, of which some represent one thing and
some another, it is evident that they differ greatly among
themselves. For those that represent substances [32] are undoubtedly something more, and contain in themselves, so to
speak, more objective reality ⌜, or rather, participate by representation in a higher degree of being or perfection,⌝ than
those that represent only modes or accidents. Furthermore,
that by which I conceive a supreme God, eternal, infinite, ⌜im-
mutable,⌝ omniscient, omnipotent, and the universal creator of
all things that exist outside of himself—that idea, I say, certainly contains in itself more objective reality than do those
by which finite substances are represented.

Now it is obvious, according to the light of nature, that
there must be at least as much reality in the total efficient
cause as in its effect, for whence can the effect derive its
reality, if not from its cause? And how could this cause com-
municate reality to the effect, unless it possessed it in itself?

And from this it follows, not only that something cannot be
derived from nothing, but also that the more perfect—that is
to say, that which contains in itself more reality (41)—cannot
be a consequence of ⌜and dependent upon⌝ the less perfect.
This truth is not only clear and evident in regard to the ef-
fects which have ⌜what philosophers call⌝ actual or formal reality, but also in regard to the ideas where one considers only
⌜what they call⌝ objective reality. For example, the stone
which has not yet existed cannot now begin to be, unless it is
produced by a being that possesses in itself formally or eminently all that enters into the composition of stone ⌜—that is,
which contains in itself the same things as, or others more ex-
cellent than, those which are in stone⌝. Heat cannot be produced in a being that previously lacked it, unless by something which is of an order ⌜, a degree, or a type⌝ at least as
perfect as heat, and so forth. But still, in addition, the idea of
heat or of stone cannot be in me, unless it was put there by
something which contains in itself at least as much reality as I
conceive there is in heat or stone; for even though that cause

does not transfer to my idea anything of its actual or formal reality, we must not therefore suppose that such a cause is any less real, nor that the nature of an idea ⌐, since it is a work of the mind,⌐ is such that it does not require any other formal reality than what it receives and borrows from thought or mind, of which it is only a mode ⌐—that is, a way or manner of thinking⌐. In order that an idea should contain one particular objective reality rather [33] than another, it should no doubt obtain it from some cause in which there is at least as much formal reality as the idea contains objective reality. For if we suppose that there is some element in an idea which is not present in its cause, this element must then arise from nothing. However imperfect may be this mode of being, by which a thing exists objectively or is represented by a concept of it in the understanding, certainly we can nevertheless say that this mode and manner of being is not nothing, and consequently the idea cannot derive its origin from nothingness.

Nor must I imagine that, since the reality that I consider to be in my ideas is only objective, the same reality need not (42) be present formally ⌐or actually⌐ in the causes of these ideas, but that it is sufficient that it should be objectively present in them. For just as this manner of existing objectively belongs to ideas as part of their own nature, so also the manner or fashion of existing formally belongs to the causes of these ideas, or at the very least to their first and principal causes, as part of their own nature. And even though it might happen that one idea gives birth to another idea, that could not continue indefinitely; but we must finally reach a first idea, the cause of which is like an archetype ⌐or source⌐, in which is contained formally ⌐and in actuality⌐ all the reality ⌐or perfection⌐ that is found only objectively or by representation in the ideas. Thus the light of nature makes me clearly recognize that ideas in me are like paintings or pictures, which can, truly, easily fall short of the perfection of the original from which they have been drawn, but which can never contain anything greater or more perfect. And the longer and the

more carefully I consider all these arguments, the more clearly
and distinctly I know that they are true.

What, then, shall I conclude from all this evidence? Clearly,
that if the objective reality ⌈'or perfection'⌉ of some one of my
ideas is such that I recognize clearly that this same reality ⌈'or
perfection'⌉ does not exist in me, either formally or eminently, and consequently that I cannot myself be its cause, it
necessarily follows that I am not alone in the world, but that
there is also some other entity that exists and is the cause of
this idea. On the other hand, if I find no such idea in myself,
I will have no argument which can convince me and make me
certain of the existence of any entity other than myself; for I
have diligently searched for all such arguments [34] and have
been thus far unable to find any other.

Among all these ideas which exist in me, besides that which
represents myself to myself, concerning which there can be no
difficulty here, (43) there is another which represents a God,
others corporeal and inanimate things, others angels, others
animals, and still others which represent men similar to myself. But as far as the ideas which represent other men, or animals, or angels are concerned, I can easily imagine that they
could be formed by the ⌈mixture and⌉ combination of my
other ideas, 'of myself,' of corporeal objects, and of God, even
though outside of me there were no other men in the world,
nor any animals, nor any angels. And as far as the ideas of
corporeal objects are concerned, I recognize nothing in them
so great ⌈or so excellent⌉ that it seems impossible that they
could arise from myself. For if I consider them more closely
and examine them in the same way that I examined the idea of
wax yesterday, I find that there are only a few elements in them
which I conceive clearly and distinctly—namely, size, or extension in length, width and depth; shape, which results from the
termination and limitation of this extension; location, which
the variously shaped objects have with respect to one another;
and movement, or the changing of this location. To this one
may add substance, duration, and number. As for other ele-

ments, such as light, colors, sounds, odors, tastes, heat, cold, and the other qualities involved in the sense of touch, they occur in my thought with so much obscurity and confusion that I do not even know whether they are true or false and only apparent, that is, whether my ideas of these qualities are really ideas of actual bodies or of non-bodies ⌈, which are only chimerical and cannot exist⌉. For even though I have previously stated that true and formal falsity can characterize judgments only, there can exist nevertheless a certain material falsity in ideas, as when they represent that which is nothing as though it were something. For example, my ideas of cold and heat are so little clear (44) and distinct that I cannot determine from them whether cold is only the absence of heat or heat the absence of cold, or whether both of them are real qualities, or whether neither is such. Besides, ⌈since ideas are like pictures,⌉ there can be no ideas which do not [35] seem to us to represent objects; and if it is true to say that cold is nothing but an absence of heat, the idea of cold which represents it as something real and positive could, not inappropriately, be called false, and so for other similar ideas.

And assuredly, it is not necessary for me to attribute to such ideas any other source than myself. For if they are false—that is, if they represent entities which do not exist—the light of nature lets me know that they proceed from nothingness; that is, that they occur in me only because something is lacking in my nature and that the latter is not altogether perfect. And if these ideas are true, nevertheless, since they show me so little reality that I cannot even ⌈clearly⌉ distinguish the object represented from the nonexistent, I do not see why they could not be produced by myself ⌈and why I could not be their author⌉.

As for my clear and distinct ideas of corporeal things, there are some of them which, it seems to me, might have been derived from my ideas of myself, such as my ideas of substance, duration, number, and other similar things. For I think that stone is a substance, or a thing which is capable of existing by itself, and that I myself am also a substance, even though I

understand perfectly that I am a being that thinks and
that is not extended, and that stone, on the contrary, is an
extended being which does not think. Nevertheless, even
though there is a notable difference between these two conceptions, they seem to agree in this fact that both of them
represent substances. In the same way, when I think I exist
now and remember in addition having existed formerly, or
when I conceive various thoughts of which I recognize the
number, I acquire (45) the ideas of duration and number
which I afterward am able to apply to any other things I
wish. As for the other qualities of which the ideas of material
entities are composed—namely, extension, shape, location, and
movement—it is true that they are not formally in my nature,
since I am only a thinking being; but since these are only particular modes of substance, ˹or, as it were, the garments in
which corporeal substance appears to us,˺ and since I am myself a substance, it seems that they might be contained in my
nature eminently.

Thus there remains only the idea of God, in which we must
consider if there is something which could not have come
from myself. By the word "God" I mean an infinite substance,
˹eternal, immutable,˺ [36] independent, omniscient, omnipotent, and that by which I myself and all other existent things,
if it is true that there are other existent things, have been
created and produced. But these attributes are ˹such ˹—they
are˺ so great and so eminent—˺ that the more attentively I
consider them, the less I can persuade myself that I could
have derived them from my own nature. And consequently we
must necessarily conclude from all that I have previously said
that God exists. For even though the idea of substance exists
in me from the very fact that I am a substance, I would nevertheless have no idea of an infinite substance, I who am a finite
being, unless the idea had been placed in me by some substance which was in fact infinite.

And I must not imagine that I do not conceive infinity as a
real idea, but only through the negation of what is finite in
the manner that I comprehend rest and darkness as the nega-

tion of movement and light. On the contrary, I see manifestly that there is more reality in infinite substance than in finite substance, and my notion of the infinite is somehow prior to that of the finite, that is, the notion of God is prior to that of myself. For how would it be possible for me to know that I doubt and that I (46) desire—that is, that I lack something and am not all perfect—if I did not have in myself any idea of a being more perfect than my own, by comparison with which I might recognize the defects of my own nature?

And we cannot say that this idea of God might be materially false, and that in consequence I might derive it from nothingness, ⌈or, in other words, that it might be in me as a deficiency,⌉ as I have just now said about the ideas of heat and cold, and other similar things. For, on the contrary, this idea is very clear and very distinct and contains more objective reality than does any other, so that there is no other which is more true from its very nature, nor which is less open to the suspicion of error and falsity.

This idea, I say, of a supremely perfect and infinite being, is entirely true; for even though one might imagine that such a being does not exist, nevertheless one cannot imagine that the idea of it does not represent anything real, as I have just said of the idea of cold. It is also very clear and very distinct, since everything real and true which my mind conceives clearly and distinctly, and which contains some perfection, is contained and wholly included in this idea. [37] And this will be no less true even though I do not comprehend the infinite and though there is in God an infinity of things which I cannot comprehend, or even perhaps suggest in thought, for it is the nature of infinity that I, who am finite and limited, cannot comprehend it. It is enough that I understand this and that I judge that all qualities which I conceive clearly and in which I know that there is some perfection, and possibly also an infinity of other qualities of which I am ignorant, are in God formally or eminently. Then the idea which I have of God is seen to be the truest, the clearest, and the most distinct of all the ideas which I have in my mind.

But possibly I am something more than I suppose myself to be. Perhaps all the perfections which I attribute to the nature of a God are somehow potentially in me, although they ⌈are not yet actualized and⌉ do not yet appear (47) and make themselves known by their actions. Experience shows, in fact, that my knowledge increases and improves little by little, and I see nothing to prevent its increasing thus, more and more, to infinity; nor ⌈even⌉ why, my knowledge having thus been augmented and perfected, I could not thereby acquire all the other perfections of divinity; nor finally, why my potentiality of acquiring these perfections, if it is true that I possess it, should not be sufficient to produce the ideas of them ⌈and introduce them into my mind⌉.

Nevertheless, ⌈considering the matter more closely, I see that⌉ this could not be the case. For, first, even if it were true that my knowledge was always achieving new degrees of perfection and that there were in my nature many potentialities which had not yet been actualized, nevertheless none of these qualities belong to or approach ⌈in any way⌉ my idea of divinity, in which nothing is merely potential ⌈and everything is actual and real⌉. Is it not even a most certain ⌈and infallible⌉ proof of the imperfection of my knowledge that it can ⌈grow little by little and⌉ increase by degrees? Furthermore, even if my knowledge increased more and more, I am still unable to conceive how it could ever become actually infinite, since it would never arrive at such a high point of perfection that it would no longer be capable of acquiring some still greater increase. But I conceive God to be actually infinite in such a high degree that nothing could be added to the ⌈supreme⌉ perfection that he already possesses. And finally, I understand ⌈very well⌉ that the objective existence of an idea can never be produced by a being that [38] is merely potential and that, properly speaking, is nothing, but only by a formal or actual being.

And certainly there is nothing in all that I have just said which is not easily known by the light of nature to all those who will consider it carefully. But when I relax my attention somewhat, my mind is obscured, as though blinded by the images of sensible objects, and does not easily recall the reason why my idea of a being more perfect than my own must necessarily have been imparted to me by a being that is actually more perfect. (48)

That is why I wish to pass on now to consider whether I myself, who have this idea of God, could exist if there had been no God. And I ask, from what source would I have derived my existence? Possibly from myself, or from my parents, or from some other causes less perfect than God; for we could ⟨think of or⟩ imagine nothing more perfect, nor even equal to him. But if I were ⌈independent of anything else and were⌉ the author of my own being, I would doubt nothing, I would experience no desires, and finally I would lack no perfection. For I would have endowed myself with all those perfections of which I had any notion, and thus I would be God ⟨himself⟩.

And I must not imagine that what I lack might be more difficult to acquire than what I already possess; for, on the contrary, it is very certain that it was far more difficult for this ego—that is, this being or substance that thinks—to emerge from nothingness than it would be for me to acquire the ⌈insight into and⌉ knowledge of various matters about which I am ignorant, since this knowledge would only be an accident of this substance. And certainly if I had given myself all the qualities that I have just mentioned and more, ⌈that is, if I were myself the author of my birth and of my being,⌉ I would at least not have denied to myself those things which could be obtained with greater facility ⌈as are an infinity of items of information, of which my nature happens to be deprived⌉. I would not even have denied myself any of the qualities which I see are included in the idea of God, because there is no one of them which seems to me to be more difficult to create or acquire. And if there were one of them which was more difficult, certainly it would have appeared so to me, because, on the assumption that all my other qualities were self-given, I would see in this one quality a limitation of my power ⌈since I would not be able to acquire it⌉.

Even if I could suppose that possibly I have always been as I am now, still I could not evade the force [39] of this argument ⟨since it would not follow that no author of my existence need then be sought ⸢and⟩ I would still have to recognize that it is necessary that God is the author of my existence⸣. For the whole duration of my life can be divided into (49) an infinite number of parts, no one of which is in any way dependent upon the others; and so it does not follow from the fact that I have existed a short while before that I should exist now, unless at this very moment some cause produces and creates me, as it were, anew or, more properly, conserves me.

Actually it is quite clear and evident to all who will consider attentively the nature of time that a substance, to be conserved at every moment that it endures, needs the same power and the same action which would be necessary to produce it and create it anew if it did not yet exist. Thus the light of nature makes us see clearly that conservation and creation differ only in regard to our manner of thinking ⸢and not in reality⸣.

It is therefore only necessary here for me to question myself and consider my own nature to see whether I possess some power and ability by means of which I can bring it about that I, who exist now, shall still exist a moment later. For since I am nothing but a being which thinks, or at least since we are so far concerned only with that part of me, if such a power resided in me, certainly I should at least be conscious of it ⸢and recognize it⸣. But I am aware of no such thing, and from that fact I recognize evidently that I am dependent upon some ⟨other⟩ being different from myself.

But possibly that being upon whom I am dependent is not God, and I am produced either by my parents or by some other causes less perfect than he. Not at all, that cannot be the case. For, as I have already said, it is very evident that there must be at least as much reality in the cause as in the effect; and since I am a being who thinks and who has some idea of God, whatever turns out to be the cause of my existence must be admitted to be also a being who thinks and which has in itself the idea of all the perfections which I attribute to ⌈the divine nature ⌐of⌐ God⌐. Thus we can in turn inquire whether this cause derives its ⌈origin and⌐ existence from itself or from something else. For if it is self-caused, it follows, for the reasons that I have previously given, that this cause must be God ⌐himself⌐, (50) since, to have the capacity to be or exist by itself, it must also, without doubt, have the power to possess in actuality all the perfections which it can imagine, that is, all those that I conceive [40] to be in God. But if it derives its existence from something else, we ask once more, for the same reason, whether this second cause is caused by itself or by another, until ⌈step by step⌐ we finally arrive at an ultimate cause which will ⌈turn out to⌐ be God. And it is very obvious that in this case there cannot be an infinite regress, since it is not so much a question of the cause which produced me in the past as of that which conserves me in the present.

Nor can we pretend that possibly several ⌐partial⌐ causes have concurred to produce me, and that from one of them I received the idea of one of the perfections which I attribute to God, and from another the idea of some other, so that each of these perfections would actually be found somewhere in the universe, but would nowhere be joined together ⌈and assembled⌐ in one entity which would be God. For, on the contrary, the unity, simplicity, or inseparability of all the qualities which are in God is one of the principal perfections which I conceive to be in him. And certainly the idea of this unity of all God's perfections could not have been placed in me by any cause from which I had not also received the ideas of all the other perfections. For nothing could have brought it about that I understood these qualities as joined together and inseparable, without having brought it about at the same time that I know what qualities they were ⌈and that I knew something about each one of them⌐.

Finally, concerning my parents, ⌈from whom it seems that I derive my birth,⌐ even if all that I could ever have believed of them should be true, that would still not imply that it is they

who conserve me, nor even that they made and produced me
in so far as I am a thinking being ⌐⌐, there being no relation
between the bodily activity by which I have been accustomed
to believe I was engendered and the production of a thinking
substance⌐. The most that they can have contributed to my
birth is that they have produced certain arrangements in the
matter within which I have so far believed that the real I,
that is, my mind, (51) is enclosed. Thus the existence of my
parents is no objection to the argument, and we must necessarily conclude from the mere fact that I exist and that I have
an idea of a supremely perfect Being, or God, that the existence of God is very clearly demonstrated.

The only task left is to consider how I received this idea
⌐from God⌐; for I did not get it through the senses, nor has it
ever appeared to me unexpectedly, as the ideas of sensible objects are wont to do, when these objects are presented or seem
to be presented [41] to my external sense organs. Nor is it
only a product ⌐or fiction⌐ of my mind, for it is not in my
power to diminish it or to add anything to it. No possibility
remains, consequently, except that this idea is born and produced with me from the moment that I was created, just as
was the idea of myself.

And truly it must not be thought strange that God, in cre-
ating me, put this idea in my nature in much the same way
as an artisan imprints his mark on his work. Nor is it necessary that this mark be something different from the work itself. From the very fact that God has created me, it is very
credible that he has made me, in some sense, in his own image
and similitude, and that I conceive this similitude, in which
the idea of God is contained, by the same faculty by which I
conceive myself. In other words, when I reflect upon myself,
I not only know that I am ⌐an imperfect being,⌐ incomplete
and dependent upon some other being, and a being which
strives and aspires incessantly to become something better and
greater than I now am, but also and at the same time I know
that the being upon which I depend possesses in itself all
these great qualities ⌐to which I aspire and the ideas of which

I find in myself, and possesses these qualities⌐, not indefinitely and merely potentially, but ⌐really,⌐ actually, and infinitely, and so that it is God. And the whole force of the argument ⌐I have here used to prove the existence of God⌐ consists in the fact that I recognize that it would not be possible (52) for my nature to be what it is, possessing the idea of a God, unless God really existed—the same God, I say, the idea of whom I possess, the God who possesses all these ⌐high⌐ perfections of which my mind can have some ⟨slight⟩ idea, without however being able fully to comprehend them; who is subject to no defect ⌐and who has no part of all those qualities which involve imperfection⌐. And from this it is quite evident that he cannot be a deceiver, since the light of nature teaches us that deception must always be the result of some deficiency.

But before I examine this more carefully and pass on to the consideration of other truths which may follow from this one, it seems proper to pause for a while to contemplate this all-perfect God, to weigh at leisure his ⌐marvelous⌐ attributes, to consider, admire, and adore the ⌐incomparable⌐ beauty of this immense magnificence, as far at least as the power of my mind, which is somewhat overwhelmed by it, permits. [42]

For just as faith teaches that the supreme felicity of the next life consists only in this contemplation of divine majesty, so let us try from now on whether a similar contemplation, although incomparably less perfect, will not make us enjoy the greatest happiness that we are capable of experiencing in this life.

# FOURTH MEDITATION

## OF THE TRUE AND THE FALSE

In these last few days I have become so accustomed to ignoring my senses, and I have so carefully noticed that we know very little (53) with certainty about corporeal things and that we know much more about the human mind, and still more again about God himself, that it is easy for me now to turn my consideration from ⌈sensible or⌉ picturable things to those which, being wholly dissociated from matter, are purely intelligible. And certainly my idea of the human mind, in so far as it is a thinking being, not extended in length, breadth, and depth, and participating in none of the qualities of body, is incomparably more distinct than my idea of anything corporeal. And when I consider that I doubt, that is to say, that I am an incomplete and dependent being, the idea of a complete and independent being, that is, of God, occurs to my mind with very great distinctness and clearness. And from the very fact that such an idea occurs in me, or that I who possess this idea exist, I so evidently conclude that God exists and that my own existence depends entirely upon him every moment of my life that I am confident that the human mind can know nothing with greater evidence and certainty. And I already seem to have discovered a path that will lead us from this contemplation of the true God, in whom all the treasures of science and wisdom are contained, to the knowledge of all other beings ⌈in the universe⌉.

For first, I recognize that it is impossible for God ever [43] to deceive me, since in all fraud and deception there is some kind of imperfection. And although it seems that to be able to deceive is a mark of ⟨acumen,⟩ ⌈subtlety,⌉ or power, nevertheless to wish to deceive testifies without question to weakness or malice, which could not be found in God.

Then, I know by my own experience that I have some ability to judge, ⌈⟨or to distinguish the true from the false,⟩⌉ an ability which I have no doubt received from God just as I have received all the other qualities ⟨which are part of me ⌈and⟩ which I possess⌉. (54) Furthermore, since it is impossible that God wishes to deceive me, it is also certain that he has not given me an ability of such a sort that I could ever go wrong when I use it properly.

And no doubt on this subject would remain, except that we could apparently then draw the conclusion that I can never commit an error. For if everything in me is derived from God, and if he has not given me any ability to make errors, it seems that I should never be mistaken. It is true that when I consider ⌐'myself'⌐ only ⌐'as a creature of'⌐ God, 'and when I orient myself completely upon him,' I discover ⌐in myself⌐ no cause of error or falsity. But when, a little later, I think of myself, experience convinces me that I am nevertheless subject to innumerable errors. And when I try to discover the reason for this, I notice that there is present in my thought not only a real and positive idea of God, or rather of a supremely perfect being, but also, so to speak, a certain negative idea of nothingness, or of what is infinitely removed from every kind of perfection. And I see that I am, as it were, a mean between God and nothingness, that is, so placed between the supreme Being and not-being that, in so far as a supreme Being has produced me, there is truly nothing in me which could lead me into error; but if I consider myself as somehow participating in nothingness or not-being, that is, in so far as I am not myself the supreme being 'and am lacking many things', ⌐I find myself exposed to an infinity of defects, so that⌐ I should not be astonished if I go wrong.

Thus I 'clearly' recognize that error as such is not something real which depends upon God, but only a deficiency. Thus, in order to err, I do not need a faculty [1] which God has given to me expressly for the purpose; mistakes on my part occur because the power that God has given me to discriminate between the true and the false is not infinite.

Nevertheless I am not yet altogether satisfied, for error is not (55) a pure negation ⌐—that is, it is not a simple deficiency or lack of some perfection which is not my [44] due⌐, but rather a privation 'or lack' of some knowledge which it seems to me that I should possess. And in considering the nature of God, it does not seem possible that he should have endowed me with any faculty [2] which is not perfect of its kind, or which

[1] [L. *facultas;* F. *puissance.*]
[2] [L. *facultas;* F. *faculté.*]

lacks some perfection which is its due. For if it is true that the more expert the artisan, the more perfect ⌜and finished⌝ the artifacts produced by his hands, what could ⌜we imagine to⌝ have been produced by this supreme creator of the universe that is not ⌜perfect and⌝ entirely complete in all its parts? Certainly there is no doubt but that God could have created me such that I would never be mistaken; it is also certain that he always wills that which is best. Is it therefore a better thing to ⌜be able to⌝ make a mistake than not to ⌜be able to⌝ do so?

Considering this question with attention, it occurs to me, to begin with, that I should not be astonished at not being able to understand why God does what he does; and that I must not for this reason doubt his existence, since I may perchance observe in my experience many other beings that exist, even though I cannot understand why or how they were made. For, knowing by now that my nature is extremely weak and limited and that God's, on the contrary, is immense, incomprehensible, and infinite, I no longer have any difficulty in recognizing that there are an infinity of things within his power the causes of which lie beyond the powers of my mind. And this consideration alone is sufficient to persuade me that all causes of the type we are accustomed to call final are useless in physical ⌜or natural⌝ affairs, for it does not seem possible for me, without presumption, to seek and undertake to discover the ⌜impenetrable⌝ purposes of God.

Furthermore, it occurs to me that we should not consider a single creation separately when we investigate whether the works of God are perfect, but generally all created objects together. For the same thing which might perhaps, with some sort of justification, appear to be very imperfect if it were alone in the world (56) is seen to be very perfect when considered as constituting a part of this whole universe. And although, since I undertook to doubt everything, I have so far only learned with certainty of my existence and of God's, nevertheless, since I have recognized the infinite power of God, I could not deny that he has produced many other things, or at least that he could produce them, in such a way that I exist and am placed in the world as forming a part of the universality of all beings. [45]

Consequently, when I come to examine myself more closely and to consider what are my errors, which alone testify that there is imperfection in me, I find that they depend upon two joint causes, namely, the faculty of knowing which I possess and the faculty of choice, or rather of free will—that is to say, of my understanding together with my will. For by the understanding alone ⌈I neither assert nor deny anything, but⌉ I only conceive the ideas of things which I may assert or deny. Nor ⌈in considering the understanding thus precisely⌉ can we say that any error is ever found in it, provided that we take the word "error" in its proper sense. And even if there might be in the world an infinity of things of which my understanding has no idea, we cannot therefore say that it is deprived of these ⌈ideas as of something which is owed to its nature⌉, but only that it does not possess them, because in reality there is no argument which can prove that God ought to have given me a greater ⌈and more ample⌉ faculty of knowing than what he has given me; and however adroit ⌈and able⌉ a worker I consider him to be, I must not therefore think that he ought to have put in each of his works all the perfections which he is able to bestow upon some. Thus I cannot complain because God has not given me a sufficiently ample and perfect free will or volition, since ⌈, as a matter of fact,⌉ I experience ⌈it to be so ample and extended⌉ that there are no limits which restrict it.

And it appears to me to be very remarkable that, of all the other qualities which I possess, there is none (57) so perfect or so great that I do not ⌈clearly⌉ recognize that it could be even greater or more perfect. Thus for example, if I consider my faculty of conceiving, I ⌈immediately⌉ recognize that it is of very small extent and greatly limited; and at the same time there occurs to me the idea of another faculty, much more ample, ⌜indeed immensely greater⌝ and even infinite, and from

the very fact that I can imagine this I recognize ⌐without diffi-
culty⌐ that it belongs to the nature of God. In the same way,
if I examine memory, imagination, or any other faculty of
mine, I find no one of them which is not quite small and
limited and which is not, in God, immense ⌐and infinite⌐.
There is only volition alone, ⸝or the liberty of the ⌐free⌐ will,⸍
which I experience to be so great in myself that I cannot conceive the idea of any other more ⌐ample and⌐ extended, so
that this is what principally indicates to me that I am made
in the image and likeness of God. For even though the will
may be incomparably greater in God than in myself, either
because of the [46] knowledge and the power which are joined
with it and which make it surer and more efficacious, or because of its object, since it extends to infinitely more things,
nevertheless it does not appear any greater when I consider it
formally and precisely by itself. For it consists only in the fact
that we can ⌐make a choice; we can⌐ do a given thing or not
do it—that is to say, we can affirm or deny, pursue or avoid.
Or more properly, our free will consists only in the fact that
in affirming or denying, pursuing or avoiding the things sug-
gested by the understanding, we behave in such a way that we
do not feel that any external force has constrained us in our
decision.

For in order to be free, it is not necessary for me to be indifferent about the choice of one or the other of the two con-
traries, but rather, the more I lean to one, either because I
see clearly that it contains ⸝the preponderance (58) of⸍ both
goodness and truth or because God so guides my private
thoughts, the more freely do I choose ⌐and embrace⌐ it. And
certainly, divine grace and natural understanding, far from
diminishing my liberty, rather augment and strengthen it.
Moreover, that indifference which I feel when I am not more
moved toward one side than the other by ⌐the weight of⌐ some
reason is the lowest degree of liberty, and is rather a defect
in the understanding than a perfection of the will. For if I always understood clearly what is true and what is good, I

would never need to deliberate about what judgment and what choice I ought to make, and so I would be entirely free without ever being indifferent.

From all this I recognize, on the one hand, that the cause of my errors is not the power of willing ⸤considered by itself⸥, which I have received from God, for it is very ample and perfect in its own kind. Nor, on the other hand, is it the power of ⸢understanding or⸣ conceiving; for since I conceive nothing except by means of this power which God has given me in order to conceive, no doubt everything I conceive I conceive properly, and it is not possible for me to be deceived in that respect.

Whence, then, do my errors arise? Only from the fact that the will is ⸢much⸣ more ample and far-reaching than the understanding, so that I do not restrain it within the same limits but extend it even to those things which I do not understand. Being ⸢by its nature⸣ indifferent about such matters, it very easily is turned aside from the true and the good ⸢and chooses the false and the evil⸣. And thus it happens that I make mistakes and that I sin.

For example, when I recently examined the question whether anything in the world existed, and I recognized from the very fact that I examined [47] this question that it was very evident that I myself existed, I could not refrain from concluding that what I conceived so clearly was true. Not that I found myself forced to this conclusion by any (59) external cause, but only because the great clarity which was in my understanding produced a great inclination of my will, and I was led to this conviction all the more ⸤spontaneously and⸥ freely as I experienced in myself less indifference. Now, on the contrary, I know not only that I exist, in so far as I am something that thinks, but there is also present in my mind a certain idea of corporeal nature. In consequence, I wonder whether this nature that thinks, which is in me, or rather which is myself, is different from this corporeal nature, or if both are one and the same. I am supposing, here, that I do not yet know any argument to convince me of one possibility

rather than the other, so it follows that I am entirely indifferent as to denying or affirming it, or even as to abstaining from
making any judgment.

And this indifference extends not only to those things with
which the understanding has no acquaintance, but also to all
those generally that it does not comprehend with ⌐sufficient
⌐-ly˺ perfect⌐ clarity at the moment when the will is deliber-
ating the issue. For however probable may be the conjectures
which incline me to a particular judgment, the mere recogni-
tion that they are only conjectures and not certain and indubitable reasons is enough to give me grounds for making
the contrary judgment. I have had sufficient experience of this
in these past few days when I assumed as false all that I had
previously held to be very true, merely because I noticed that
it was somehow possible to doubt it.

Now, if I abstain from making a judgment upon a topic
when I do not conceive it sufficiently clearly and distinctly, it
is evident that I do well and am not making a mistake; but if
I decide to deny or affirm it, then I am not making a proper
use of my free will. And (60) if in this situation I affirm what
is not true, it is evident that I am making a mistake; and even
when I judge according to the truth, it is only by chance, and
I am not for that reason free of blame ⌐for misusing my free-
dom⌐. For the light of nature dictates that the understanding
should always know before the will makes a decision.

It is in this improper use of the free will that we find the
privation which [48] constitutes the essence of error. Privation, I say, is found in the operation in so far as it proceeds
from me, but not in the faculty which I have received from
God, nor even in the operation in so far as it depends upon
him. For certainly I have no reason to complain because God
has not given me a more ample intelligence or a more perfect
insight than what he has bestowed upon me, since it is ⌐actu-
ally⌐ the nature of a finite understanding not to comprehend
many things, and it is the nature of a created understanding
to be finite. On the contrary, far from conceiving such unjust
sentiments as to imagine that he has deprived me or unjustly

kept from me the other perfections with which he has not endowed me, I have every reason to give him thanks because,
never having any obligation to me, he has nevertheless given
me those ⌈few⌉ perfections that I have.

Nor have I any reason to complain because he has given me
a volition more ample than my understanding. For as the
volition consists of just one body, ⌈its subject being⌉ apparently indivisible, it seems that its nature is such that nothing
could be taken from it without destroying it. And, certainly,
the more ample it is, the more reason I have to give thanks
for the generosity of the One who has given it to me.

Nor, finally, have I any reason to complain that God con-
curs with me to perform the acts of this volition, that is, the
judgments in which I am mistaken. For those acts are entirely
true and absolutely good in so far as they depend upon God,
and there is somehow more perfection in my nature because I
can perform them than there would be if I could not. As for
privation, in which alone is found the formal cause (61) of
error and sin, it has no need of any concurrence on the part
of God, since it is not a thing ⌈or a being⌉ and since, if it is
referred to God as to its cause, it should not be called privation but only negation ⌈according to the significance attached
to these words in the schools⌉. For actually it is not an imperfection in God that he has given me the liberty of ⌈judging or
not judging, ⌟or⌞ giving or withholding my assent,⌝ on certain
matters of which he has given me no clear and distinct knowledge. It is, without doubt, an imperfection in myself not to
make proper use of this liberty, and ⌈rashly⌉ to pass judgment
on matters which I ⌟do not rightly understand ⌈and⌝ conceive
only obscurely and confusedly⌉.

I perceive, nevertheless, that it would have been easy for
God to contrive that I would never make mistakes, even
though I remained free and with limited knowledge. He
might, for example, have given my understanding [49] a clear
and distinct comprehension of all the things about which I
should ever deliberate, or he might simply have engraved so
deeply in my memory the resolution never to pass judgment

on anything without conceiving it clearly and distinctly that
I could never forget this rule. And I ʿreadilyˑ recognize ʿin so
far as I possess the comprehension of any whole,ˑ that ʿwhen I
consider myself alone, as if I were the only person in the
world,ˑ I would have been ʿmuchˑ more perfect than I am if
God had so created me ʿthat I never made a mistakeˑ; nevertheless I cannot therefore deny that the universe may be somehow more perfect because some of its parts are not free from
defect ʿwhile others areˑ, than it would be if all its parts were
alike.

And I have no right to complain because God, having put
me in the world, has not wished to place me in the ranks of
the noblest and most perfect beings. ʿI indeed have reason to
rejoice because,ˑ even if I do not have the power of avoiding
error by the first method ʿwhich I have just describedˑ, which
depends upon a clear and evident knowledge of all the things
about which I can deliberate, the other method, at least, is
within my power. This is, (62) firmly to adhere to the resolution never to pass judgment upon things whose truth is not
clearly known to me. For even though I experience in myself
the weakness of not being able to keep my mind continuously
faithful to a fixed resolution, I can nevertheless, by attentive
and frequently repeated meditation, so strongly impress it
upon my memory that I will never fail to recollect it whenever there is need, and thus I can acquire the habit of not
erring. And since this comprises the greatest and principal
perfection of man, I consider that I have benefited not a little
by today's meditation, in having discovered the cause of error
and falsity.

And certainly, there can be no other cause than the one I
have just explained, for whenever I restrict my volition within
the bounds of my knowledge, whenever my volition makes no
judgment except upon matters clearly and distinctly reported
to it by the understanding, it cannot happen that I err. For
every clear and distinct conception is without doubt something ʿreal and positiveˑ, and thus cannot derive its origin
from nothingness, but must have God for its author—God, I

say, who, [50] being supremely perfect, cannot be the cause of any error—and consequently we must conclude that such a conception ⌈or such a judgment⌉ is true.

For the rest, I have not only learned today what I must avoid in order not to err, but also what I ought to do to arrive at the knowledge of the truth. For I shall certainly achieve this goal if I hold my attention sufficiently fixed upon all those things which I conceive perfectly and if I distinguish these from the others which I conceive only confusedly and obscurely. And from now on I shall take particular care to act accordingly. (63)

# FIFTH MEDITATION

## OF THE ESSENCE OF MATERIAL THINGS AND, ONCE MORE, OF GOD: THAT HE EXISTS

There are many other questions for me to inquire into concerning the attributes of God and concerning my own nature, or the nature of my mind. I may, perhaps, pursue this investigation some other time; for the present, having noticed what must be done or avoided in order to arrive at the knowledge of the truth, my principal task is to attempt to escape from ⌈and relieve myself of all⌉ the doubts into which I have fallen in these last few days, and to see if we cannot know anything certain about material objects. But before examining whether such objects exist outside of myself, I must consider the concepts of these objects, in so far as they occur in my thought, and see which of them are distinct and which of them are confused.

In the first place, I picture distinctly that quantity which philosophers commonly call the "continuum," or extension in length, width, and depth which exists in this quantity, or rather in the body to which we attribute it. Furthermore, I

can distinguish in it various different parts and attribute to
each of these parts all sorts of sizes, shapes, positions, and
movements; and, finally, I can assign to each of these movements all degrees of duration.

And I not only know these things distinctly when I consider
them thus in general, but also, ⌐however little I am⌐ applying
my attention to it, I ⌐⸌come to⸍⌐ recognize an infinity of details concerning [51] numbers, shapes, movements, and other
similar things, the truth of which makes itself so apparent (64)
and accords so well with my nature that when I discover them
for the first time it does not seem ⌐to me⌐ as though I were
learning anything new, but rather as though I were remem-
bering what I had previously known—that is, that I am perceiving things which were already in my mind, even though
I had not yet focussed my attention upon them.

And what I believe to be more important here is that I find
in myself an infinity of ideas of certain things which cannot
be assumed to be pure nothingness, even though they may
perhaps have no existence outside of my thought. These
things are not figments of my imagination, even though it is
within my power to think of them or not to think of them;
on the contrary, they have their own true and immutable natures. Thus, for example, when I imagine a triangle, even
though there may perhaps be no such figure anywhere in the
world outside of my thought, nor ever have been, nevertheless the figure cannot help having a certain determinate nature, or form, or essence, which is immutable and eternal,
which I have not invented and which does not in any way
depend upon my mind. This is evidenced by the fact that we
can demonstrate various properties of this triangle, namely,
that its three angles are equal to two right angles, that the
greatest angle subtends the longest side, and other similar
properties. Whether I wish it or not, I ⸌now⸍ recognize ⌐very⌐
clearly ⌐and evidently⌐ that these are properties of the triangle, even though I had never previously thought of them
in any way when I first imagined one. And therefore it cannot be said that I have ⌐imagined or⌐ invented them.

Nor can I raise the objection here that possibly this idea of the triangle came to my mind ⟨from external things⟩ through the medium of my senses, since I have sometimes seen triangularly shaped objects; for I can picture in my mind an infinity of other shapes such that I cannot have the least suspicion that they have ever been present to my senses, and I am still (65) no less able to demonstrate various properties about their nature than I am about that of the triangle. These properties, certainly, must be wholly true, since I conceive them clearly. And thus they are something, and not pure negation, since it is quite evident that everything which is true is something ⌈, as truth is the same as being⟩⌉. I have already amply demonstrated that everything that I recognize clearly and [52] distinctly is true; and even if I had not demonstrated this, the nature of my mind is such that I can ⟨nevertheless⟩ not help believing things to be true while I am conceiving them clearly ⌈and distinctly⌉. And I recollect that even when I was still strongly attached to the objects of sense, I numbered among the most constant truths that which I conceived clearly ⌈and distinctly⌉ about the shapes, numbers, and other properties which belong to the fields of arithmetic and geometry ⟨or, in general, to pure and abstract mathematics⟩.

Now, if from the very fact that I can derive from my thoughts the idea of something, it follows that all that I clearly and distinctly recognize as characteristic of this thing does in reality characterize it, can I not derive from this an argument which will ⌈demonstratively⌉ prove the existence of God? It is certain that I find in my mind the idea of God, of a supremely perfect Being, no less than that of any shape or number whatsoever; and I recognize that an ⌈actual and⌉ eternal existence belongs to his nature no less clearly and distinctly than I recognize that all I can demonstrate about some figure or number actually belongs to the nature of that figure or number. Thus, even if everything that I concluded in the preceding Meditations were ⟨by chance⟩ not true, the existence of God should pass in my mind as at least as certain (66) as I have hitherto considered all the truths of mathematics ⌐, which deal only with numbers and figures⌐.

And this is true even though I must admit that it does not at first appear entirely obvious, but seems to have some appearance of sophistry. For since in all other matters I have become accustomed to make a distinction between existence and essence, I am easily convinced that the existence of God can be separated from his essence, and that thus I can conceive of God as not actually existing. Nevertheless, when I consider this with more attention, I find it manifest that we can no more separate the existence of God from his essence than we can separate from the essence of a ⌐rectilinear⌐ triangle the fact that the size of its three angles equals two right angles, or from the idea of a mountain the idea of a valley. Thus it is no less self-contradictory to conceive of a God, a supremely perfect Being, who lacks existence—that is, who lacks some perfection—than it is to conceive of a mountain for which there is no valley.

But even though in fact I cannot conceive of a God without existence, any more than of a mountain without a valley, nevertheless, just as from the mere fact that I conceive a mountain with a valley, it does not [53] follow that any mountain exists in the world, so likewise, though I conceive of God as existing, it does not seem to follow for this reason that God exists. For my thought does not impose any necessity upon things; and just as I can at my pleasure imagine a winged horse, even though no horse has wings, so I could perhaps attribute existence to God, even though no God existed.

⌐This is far from the truth;⌐ it is here that there is sophistry hidden ⌐under the guise of a valid objection⌐. For from the fact that I cannot conceive a mountain without a valley it does not follow that there is a mountain or a valley anywhere ⌐in the world⌐, but only that the mountain (67) and the valley, whether they exist or not, are inseparable from each other. From the fact alone that I cannot conceive God except as existing, it follows that existence is inseparable from him, and consequently that he does, in truth, exist. Not that my thought can bring about this result or that it imposes any necessity upon things; on the contrary, the necessity which is in the thing itself—that is, the necessity of the existence of God— determines me to have this thought. For it is not in my power to conceive of a God without existence—that is to say, of a supremely perfect Being without a supreme perfection—as it is in my power to imagine a horse either with or without wings.

And it must not be said here that it is only necessary that I admit that God exists after I have supposed that he possesses all sorts of perfections, since existence is one of them, but that my first supposition was not really necessary. Thus it is not necessary to think that all four-sided figures can be inscribed in a circle; but if we suppose that I do have this idea, I am forced to admit that a rhombus can be inscribed in one, ⌈since it is a four-sided figure,⌉ and ⌈by⌉ this ⌈I will be forced to admit what⌉ is ʼclearlyˋ false. We must not, I say, argue thus; for even though it is not necessary that I should ever have any thought about God, nevertheless, whenever I do choose to think of a first and supreme being and to derive ⌈, so to speak,⌉ the idea of God from the treasure house of my mind, it is necessary that I attribute to him all kinds of perfections, even though it does not occur to me to mention them all and to pay attention to each one of them severally. And this necessity is enough to bring it about that afterward, as soon as I come to recognize that existence is a perfection, I conclude ʼvery properlyˋ that this first and supreme Being ⌈truly⌉ exists; just as it is not necessary that I should ever imagine any triangle, but [54] every time that I wish to consider a rectilinear figure containing three angles only, it is absolutely necessary that I attribute to it everything that leads (68) to the conclusion that these three angles are not greater than two right angles, even if perhaps I do not then consider this matter in particular. But when I wish to determine what figures can be inscribed in a circle, it is in no way necessary that I think that all four-sided figures are of this number; on the contrary, I cannot even pretend that this is the case as long as I do not wish to accept anything but what I can conceive clearly and distinctly. Consequently, there is a vast difference between false suppositions, such as this one, and the true ideas which are inborn in me, of which the first and chief one is that of God. For actually I have several reasons for recognizing that this idea is not something ⌈imaginary or⌉ fictitious, depending only on my thought, but that it is the image of a true and immutable nature. The first reason is that I cannot conceive anything but God alone, to whose essence existence belongs ⌈with necessity⌉. Another reason is that it is not possible for me to conceive ⌈in the same way⌉ two or more gods ⟨such as he⟩. Again, assuming that there is now a God who exists, I see clearly that he must have existed before from all eternity and that he should be eternally in the future. And a final reason is that I conceive various other qualities in God, of which I can neither diminish nor change a particle.

For the rest, whatever proof or argument I use, I must always come back to this conclusion: that it is only the things that I conceive clearly and distinctly which have the power to convince me completely. And although among the things which I conceive in this way there are, in truth, some which are obvious ⌈-ly known⌉ to everyone, while others of them only become known to those who consider them more closely and examine them more carefully, nevertheless, after they have once been discovered, none of them can be esteemed less certain than the rest. Thus, for example, in every right-angled triangle, even though it is not so readily apparent (69) that the square of the hypotenuse is equal to the squares of the other two sides as it is that this hypotenuse is opposite the greatest angle, nevertheless, after this fact has once been recognized, we are as much convinced of the truth of the one proposition as of the other. And as for the question of God, certainly, if my mind were not prejudiced and if my thought were not distracted by the ⌈constant⌉ presence ⟨on all sides⟩ of images of sensible objects, [55] there would be nothing that I would recognize sooner or more easily than God. For is there

anything ⌈clearer and⌉ more obvious in itself than ⌈to think⌉
that there is a God, ⌈that is to say,⌉ a supreme ⌈and perfect⌉
Being, in whom ⟨uniquely⟩ ⌈necessary for eternal⌉ existence is
included in essence, and who consequently exists?

And although, in order thoroughly to understand this truth,
I have had to make a great mental effort, nevertheless I find
myself at present not only as certain of this as of everything
which seems to me most certain, but even beyond that I notice that the certainty of all other things depends upon this
so ⌈absolutely⌉ that, without this knowledge, it is impossible
ever to be able to know anything perfectly.

For even though my nature is such that as soon as I understand anything very clearly and very distinctly I cannot help
but believe it to be true, nevertheless, because I am also of
such a nature that I cannot always confine my attention to
one thing and frequently remember having judged a thing to
be true when I have ceased considering the reasons which
forced me to that conclusion, it can happen at such a time
that other reasons occur to me which would easily make me
change my mind if I did not know that there was a God. And
so I would never have true and certain knowledge concerning
anything at all, but only vague and fluctuating opinions.

Thus, for example, when I consider the nature of the ⌈⟨rec-
tilinear⟩⌉ triangle, I recognize ⟨most⟩ evidently, I, who am
somewhat skilled in geometry, that its three angles are equal
to two right angles; nor can I disbelieve this while I am pay-
ing attention to (70) its demonstration. But as soon as I turn
my attention away from the demonstration, even while I remember having clearly understood it, it can easily happen
that I doubt its truth, if I do not know that there is a God.
For I can persuade myself that I was so made by nature that
I could easily make mistakes, even in those matters which I
believe I understand with the greatest evidence ⌈and cer-
tainty⌉, especially because I remember having often judged
many things true and certain, which, later, other reasons constrained me to consider absolutely false.

But after having recognized that there is a God, and having recognized at the same time that all things are dependent upon him and that he is not a deceiver, I can infer as a consequence that everything which I conceive clearly and distinctly is necessarily true. Therefore, even if I am no longer thinking of the reasons why [56] I have judged something to be true, provided only I remember having understood it clearly and distinctly, there can never be a reason on the other side which can make me consider the matter doubtful. Thus I have ⌐a⌐ true and certain ⌐body of⌐ knowledge ʼon this matterʼ. And this same ⌐body of⌐ knowledge extends also to all the other things which I remember having formerly demonstrated, such as the truths of geometry and other similar matters. For what reason can anyone give to make me doubt them? Would it be that my nature is such that I am ⌐very likely to be⌐ ʼfrequentlyʼ deceived? But I know already that I cannot go wrong in judgments for which I clearly know the reasons. Would it be that I have formerly considered many things true and certain which I later recognized to be false? But I had not clearly or distinctly known any of those things; and not yet knowing this rule by which I am certain of truth, I had been led to believe them by reasons that I have since recognized to be less strong than I had then imagined them. What further objections could be raised? Would it be that possibly I am asleep, as I had myself argued earlier, or that all the thoughts that I now have are no more true than the dreams we imagine when asleep? But ʼeven so, nothing would be altered. Forʼ (71) even if I were asleep, all that appears evident to my mind is absolutely true.

And thus I recognize very clearly that the certainty and truth of all knowledge depends solely on the knowledge of the true God, so that before I knew him I could not know any other thing perfectly. And now that I know him, I have the means of acquiring ʼclear and certain ⌐andʼ perfect⌐ knowledge about an infinity of things, not only about God himself ʼand about other intellectual mattersʼ, but also about ⌐that which pertains to⌐ corporeal nature, in so far as it can be the object of ⸜pure mathematics ⌐—that is, of⸝ the demonstrations of geometricians who are not concerned with its existence⌐. [57]

# SIXTH MEDITATION

## OF THE EXISTENCE OF CORPOREAL THINGS AND OF THE REAL DISTINCTION BETWEEN THE MIND AND BODY ⌐OF MAN⌐

Nothing more is now left for me to do except to examine whether corporeal things exist; and I already know ⌐for certain⌐ that they can exist at least in so far as they are considered as the objects ⸜of pure mathematics, ⌐or⸝ of the demonstrations of geometry,⌐ since I conceive them in this way very clearly and very distinctly. For there is no doubt but that God has the power of producing everything that I am able to conceive with distinctness; and I have never supposed that it was impossible for him to do anything, except only when I found a contradiction in being able to conceive it well. Furthermore, my faculty of imagination, which I find by experience that I use when I apply myself to the consideration of material objects, is capable of persuading me of their existence. For when I consider attentively what the imagination is, (72) I find that it is nothing else than a particular application of the faculty of knowledge to a body which is intimately present to it and which therefore exists.

And to make this ⌐very⌐ obvious, I take note of the difference between imagination and pure intellection ⌐or conception⌐. For example, when I imagine a triangle, not only do I conceive that it is a figure composed of three lines, but along with that I envision these three lines as present, by the force ⌐and the internal effort⌐ of my mind; and it is just this that I call "imagination." But if I wish to think of a chiliogon, I recognize quite well, indeed, that it is a figure composed of a thousand sides, as easily as I conceive that a triangle is a figure composed of ⌈only⌉ three sides, but I cannot imagine the thousand sides ⌈of a chiliogon as I can the three of a triangle, nor, so to speak, look at them⌉ as though they were present ⌈to the eyes of my mind⌉. And although, following my habit of always using my imagination when I think of corporeal things, it may happen that in conceiving a chiliogon I confusedly picture some figure to myself, nevertheless it is ⌈quite⌉ evident that this figure is not a chiliogon, since it is in no way different from what I would picture to myself if I thought of a myriogon or of some other figure of many sides, and that it in no way serves [58] to bring out the properties which constitute the difference between the chiliogon and the other polygons. But if it is a question of considering a pentagon, ⌈it is quite true that⌉ I can conceive its shape, just as well as that of a chiliogon, without the aid of the imagination; but I can also imagine it by applying my mind attentively to each of its five sides, and ⌈at the same time⌉ ⌈collectively⌉ to the area ⌈or space⌉ that they enclose.

Thus I recognize clearly that I have need of a special (73) mental effort in order to imagine, which I do not require in order to ⌈conceive ⌈or⌉ understand⌉, and this ⌈special⌉ mental effort clearly shows the difference that exists between imagination and pure intellection ⌈or conception⌉. In addition, I notice that this ability to imagine which I possess, in so far as it differs from the power of conceiving, is in no way necessary to my ⌈nature or⌉ essence, that is to say, to the essence of my mind. For even if I did not possess it, there is no doubt that I would still remain the same person I now am, from which it seems to follow that it depends upon something other than my mind. And I readily conceive that if some body exists with which my mind is so joined ⌈and united⌉ that it can consider it whenever it wishes, it could be that by this means it imagines corporeal things. Thus this method of thinking only differs from pure intellection in that the mind, in conceiving, turns somehow toward itself and considers some one of the ideas which it possesses in itself, whereas in imagining it turns toward the body and considers in the latter something conformable to the idea which it has either thought of by itself or perceived through the senses. I easily conceive, I say, that the imagination can work in this fashion, if it is true that there are bodies; and because I cannot find any other way in which this can be explained ⟨equally well⟩, I therefore conjecture that bodies probably exist. But this is only a probability; and although I carefully consider all aspects of the question, I nevertheless do not see that from this distinct idea of corporeal nature which I find in my imagination, I can derive any argument which necessarily proves the existence of any body. (74)

But I have become accustomed to imagine many other things besides that corporeal nature which is the object of ⟨pure mathematics ⌐or⌐ geometry⌐, although less distinctly, such as colors, sounds, tastes, pain, and other similar qualities. And inasmuch as I perceive those qualities much better by the senses, through the medium of which, with the help of the memory, they seem to have reached my imagination, [59] I believe that in order to examine them more readily it is appropriate to consider at the same time the nature of the sensation and to see whether, from those ideas which are perceived by the method of thinking which I call "sensation," I will not be able to derive some certain proof of the existence of corporeal things.

First, I shall recall in my memory what are the things which I formerly held to be true because I had received them through the senses, and what were the bases on which my belief was founded. Afterward I shall examine the reasons which since then have obliged me to consider them doubtful, and finally, I shall consider what I ought now to believe ⟨about them⟩.

First, then, I felt that I had a head, hands, feet, and ⌐all the⌐ other members which compose this body which I thought of as a part, or possibly even as the whole, of myself. Furthermore, I felt that this body was one of a world of bodies, from

which it was capable of receiving various advantages and disadvantages; and I identified these advantages by a certain feeling of pleasure ⌈or enjoyment⌉, and the disadvantages by a
feeling of pain. Besides this pleasure and pain, I also experienced hunger, thirst, and other similar appetites, as well as
certain bodily tendencies toward gaiety, sadness, anger, and
other similar emotions. And externally, in addition to the extension, shapes, and (75) movements of bodies, I observed in
them hardness, warmth, and ⌈all the⌉ other qualities perceived
by touch. Furthermore, I noticed in them light, colors, odors,
tastes, and sounds, the variety of which enabled me to distinguish the sky, the earth, the sea, and ⌈, in general, all⌉ other
bodies, one from another.

And certainly, considering the ideas of all these qualities
which were presented to my mind [1] and which alone I directly
sensed, in the true significance of that term, it was not without reason that I believed I had sensory knowledge of things
entirely different from my thought—of bodies, namely, from
which these ideas came. For I was aware that these ideas occurred without the necessity of my consent, so that I could
not perceive any object, however much I wished, unless it was
present to one of my sense organs; nor was it in my power
not to perceive it when it was present. [60] And because the
ideas I received through the senses were much more vivid,
more detailed, and even in their own way more distinct than
any of those which I could picture to myself ⌐with conscious
purpose⌐ while meditating, or even than those which I found
impressed upon my memory, it seemed that they could not be
derived from my own mind, and therefore they must have
been produced in me by some other things. Of these things I
have no knowledge ⌐whatsoever,⌐ except that derived from the
ideas themselves, so nothing else could occur to my mind except that those things were similar to the ideas they caused.
And since I remembered that I had used my senses earlier
than my reason, and since I recognized that the ideas I formed
by myself were not as detailed as those I received through the

---

[1] [L. *cogitatio;* F. *pensée.*]

senses and were most commonly composed of the latter as parts, I easily became persuaded that I had no idea in my mind which I had not previously acquired through my senses.

It was also not without reason that I believed that this body, which by a certain particular privilege I called mine, (76) belonged to me more ⌜properly and strictly⌝ than any other. For in fact I could never be separated from it, as I could be from other bodies; I felt in it and for it all my appetites and all my emotions; and finally I experienced ⌜the sensations of⌝ pain and ⌐the thrill of⌐ pleasure in its parts, and not in those of other bodies which are separated from it.

But when I inquired why any particular sensation of pain should be followed by unhappiness in the mind and the thrill of pleasure should give rise to happiness, or even why a particular feeling of the stomach, which I call hunger, makes us want to eat, and the dryness of the throat makes us want to drink, and so on, I could give no reason except that nature teaches me so. For there is certainly no affinity ⌜and no relationship⌝, or at least none that I ⌜can⌝ understand, between the feeling in the stomach and the desire to eat, no more than between the perception of the object which causes pain and the feeling of displeasure produced by it. And in the same way, it seemed to me that I had learned from nature all the other beliefs which I held about the objects of my senses, since I noticed that the judgments I habitually made about these objects took form in my mind before I had the opportunity to weigh ⌜and consider⌝ any reasons which could oblige me to make them. [61]

Later on, various experiences gradually destroyed all my faith in my senses. For I often observed that towers which, viewed from far away, had appeared round to me, seemed at close range to be square, and that colossal statues placed on the highest summits of these towers appeared small when viewed from below. And similarly in a multitude of other experiences, I encountered errors in judgments based on the external senses. And not only on the external senses, but even on the internal ones, (77) for is there anything more intimate for more internal than pain? Yet I have learned from certain persons whose arms or legs had been amputated that it still seemed to them sometimes that they felt pain in the parts which they no longer possessed. This gives me reason to think that I could not be 'entirely' sure either that there was something wrong with one of my limbs, even though I felt a pain in it.

And to these reasons for doubting I have recently added two other very general ones. The first is that I have never thought I perceived anything when awake that I might not sometimes also think I perceived when I am asleep; and since I do not believe that the things I seem to perceive when asleep proceed from objects outside of myself, I did not see any better reason why I ought to believe this about what I seem to perceive when awake. The other reason was that, not yet knowing, or rather pretending not to know the author of my being, I saw nothing to make it impossible that I was so constructed by nature that I should be mistaken even in the things which seemed to me most true.

And as for the reasons which had previously persuaded me that sensible objects truly existed, I did not find it very difficult to answer them. For as nature seemed to lead me to many conclusions from which reason dissuaded me, I did not believe that I ought to have much faith in the teachings of this nature. And although my sense perceptions do not depend upon my volition, I did not think that I should therefore conclude that they proceeded from things different from myself, since there might perhaps be some faculty in myself even though it has been thus far unknown to me, which could [be their cause and] produce them.

But now that I am beginning to know myself better and to discover more clearly the author of my origin, I do not think in truth that I ought rashly to admit everything which the senses seem to teach us, (78) but on the other hand I do not think that I should doubt them all in general. [62]

First, since I know that all the things I conceive [2] clearly

2 [L. *intelligo;* F. *concevoir.*]

and distinctly can be produced by God exactly as I conceive them, it is sufficient that I can clearly and distinctly conceive one thing apart from another to be certain that the one is distinct ⌈or different⌉ from the other. For they can be made to exist separately, at least by ⌈the omnipotence of⌉ God, and we are obliged to consider them different no matter what power produces this separation. From the very fact that I know with certainty that I exist, and that I find that ⟨absolutely⟩ nothing else belongs ⌈necessarily⌉ to my nature or essence except that I am a thinking being, I readily conclude that my essence consists solely in being a body which thinks ⌈or a substance whose whole essence or nature is only to think⌉. And although perhaps, or rather certainly, as I will soon show, I have a body with which I am very closely united, nevertheless, since on the one hand I have a clear and distinct idea of myself in so far as I am only a thinking and not an extended being, and since on the other hand I have a distinct idea of body in so far as it is only an extended being which does not think, it is certain that this "I" ⌈—that is to say, my soul, by virtue of which I am what I am—⌉ is entirely ⌈and truly⌉ distinct from my body and that it can ⌈be or⌉ exist without it.

Furthermore, I find in myself various faculties of thinking which each have their own particular characteristics ⌈and are distinct from myself⌉. For example, I find in myself the faculties of imagination and of perception, without which I might no doubt conceive of myself, clearly and distinctly, as a whole being; but I could not ⟨, conversely,⟩ conceive of those faculties without me, that is to say, without an intelligent substance ⌈to which they are attached ⟨or⟩ in which they inhere⟩. For ⌈in our notion of them or, to use the scholastic vocabulary,⌉ in their formal concept, they embrace some type of intellection. From all this I reach the conception that these faculties are distinct from me as ⌈shapes, movements, and other⌉ modes ⌈or accidents of objects⌉ are distinct from ⌈the very⌉ objects ⌈that sustain them⌉.

I also recognize ⌈in myself⌉ some other faculties, such as the power of changing location, of assuming various postures, and

other similar ones; which cannot be conceived without some
substance in which they inhere, any more than the preceding
ones, (79) and which therefore cannot exist without such a
substance. But it is ⌐quite⌐ evident that these faculties, if
⌐it is true that⌐ they exist, must inhere in some corporeal or
extended substance, and not in an intelligent substance, since
their clear and distinct concept does actually involve some
sort of extension, but no sort of intelligence whatsoever. [63]
Furthermore, ⌐'I cannot doubt that'⌐ there is in me a certain
passive faculty of perceiving, that is, of receiving and recognizing the ideas of sensible objects; but ⌐it would be valueless
to me, and⌐ I could in no way use it if there were not ⌐also⌐
in me, or in something else, another active faculty capable of
forming and producing these ideas. But this active faculty
cannot be in me ⌐, in so far as I am a thinking being⌐, since it
does not at all presuppose ⌐my⌐ intelligence and also since
those ideas often occur to me without my contributing to
them in any way, and even ⌐frequently⌐ against my will. Thus
it must necessarily exist in some substance different from myself, in which all the reality that exists objectively in the
ideas produced by this faculty is formally or eminently contained, as I have said before. This substance is either a body—
that is, a corporeal nature—in which is formally ⌐and actually⌐
contained all that which is contained objectively ⌐and by rep-
resentation⌐ in these ideas; or else it is God himself, or some
other creation more noble than the body, in which all this is
eminently contained.

But since God is not a deceiver, it is very manifest that he
does not send me these ideas directly by his own agency, nor
by the mediation of some creation in which their ⌐objective⌐
reality does not exist formally but only eminently. For since
he has not given me any faculty for recognizing what that creation might be, but on the contrary a very great (80) inclination to believe that these ideas come from corporeal objects, I
do not see how we could clear God of the charge of deceit if
these ideas did in fact come from some other source ⌐or were
produced by other causes⌐ than corporeal objects. Therefore

we must conclude that corporeal objects exist. Nevertheless, they are not perhaps entirely what our senses perceive them to be, for there are many ways in which this sense perception is very obscure and confused; but ⌐we must¬ at least ⌐admit that¬ everything which I conceive clearly and distinctly ⌐⌐as occur-ring¬\ in them—that is to say, everything, generally speaking, which is discussed in pure ⌐mathematics ⌐or\ geometry¬—does in truth occur in them.

⌐As for the rest,\ there are other beliefs, which are very doubtful and uncertain, which are either merely particular—as, for example, that the sun is of such a size and such a shape —or else are conceived less clearly ⌐and less distinctly¬—such as light, sound, pain, and other similar things. Nevertheless, from the mere fact that God is not [64] a deceiver, and that in consequence he has not permitted any falsity in my opinions without having given me some faculty capable of correcting it, ⌐I think I can conclude with assurance that¬ I have ⌐some hope of learning the truth even about these matters ⌐and\ the means of knowing them with certainty¬.

First, there is no doubt but that all that nature teaches me contains some truth. For by nature, considered in general, I now understand nothing else but God himself, or else the ⌐order and¬ system that God has established for created things; and by my nature in particular I understand nothing else but the arrangement ⌐or assemblage¬ of all that God has given me.

Now there is nothing that this nature teaches me more ex-pressly ⌐or more obviously¬ than that I have a body which is in poor condition when I feel pain, which needs food or drink when I have the feelings of hunger or thirst, and so on. And therefore I ought to have no doubt that in this there is some truth. (81)

Nature also teaches me by these feelings of pain, hunger, thirst, and so on that I am not only residing in my body, as a pilot in his ship, but furthermore, that I am intimately con-nected with it, and that ⌐the mixture is¬ so blended ⌐, as it were,\ that ⌐something like¬ a single whole is produced. For if that were not the case, when my body is wounded I would not therefore feel pain, I, who am only a thinking being; but I would perceive that wound by the understanding alone, as a pilot perceives by sight if something in his vessel is broken. And when my body needs food or drink, I would simply know the fact itself, instead of ⌈receiving notice of it by⌉ having confused feelings of hunger and thirst. For actually all these feelings of hunger, thirst, pain, and so on are nothing else but certain confused modes of thinking, which have their origin in ⌈and depend upon⌉ the union and apparent fusion of the mind with the body.

Furthermore, nature teaches me that many other bodies exist in the vicinity of my own, of which I must seek some and avoid others. And certainly, from the fact that I perceive different kinds of colors, odors, tastes, sounds, heat, hardness, and so on, I very readily conclude that in the objects from which these various sense perceptions proceed there are some corresponding variations, although perhaps these variations are not really similar to the perceptions. And from the fact that some of these ⌈various sense⌉ perceptions are agreeable to me and others are disagreeable, [65] there is absolutely no doubt that my body, or rather my whole self, in so far as I am composed of body and mind, can in various ways be benefited or harmed by the other objects which surround it. (82)

But there are many other opinions that nature has apparently taught me which, however, I have not truly learned from her, but which were introduced into my mind by my habit of judging things inattentively. Thus it can easily happen that these opinions contain some falsity—as, for example, my opinion that all spaces in which there is nothing which ⌈affects and⌉ makes an impression on my senses are empty; that in an object which is hot there is some quality similar to my idea of heat; that in a white, ⌈or black,⌉ ⌞or green⌟ object there is the same whiteness, ⌈or blackness,⌉ ⌞or greenness⌟ that I perceive; that in a bitter or sweet object there is the same taste ⌈or the same flavor⌉, and so on for the other senses; and that stars, towers, and all other distant objects are the same shape and size that they appear ⌈from afar⌉ to our eyes, and so forth.

In order that there should be nothing in this matter that I do not conceive ⸲sufficiently⸲ distinctly, I should define ⸲more⸲ precisely what I properly mean when I say that nature teaches me something. For I am here using the word "nature" in a more restricted sense than when I use it to mean a combination ⌐or assemblage⌐ of everything God has given me, seeing that this ⌐assemblage or⌐ combination includes many things which pertain to the mind alone, to which I do not intend to refer here when speaking of nature—as ⌐for example⌐ my knowledge ⌐of this truth:⌐ that what has ⌐once⌐ been done can never ⌐after⌐ not have been done, and ⸲all ⌐of⸲ an infinity of⌐ other ⌐similar⌐ truths known to me by the light of nature ⌐without any aid of the body⌐. Such an assemblage also includes many other things which belong to body alone and are not here included under the name of "nature," such as its quality of being heavy and many other similar ones; for I am not concerned with these either, but only with those things which God has presented to me as a being composed of mind and body. This nature effectively teaches me to avoid things which produce in me the feeling of pain and to seek those which make me have some feeling of pleasure ⸲and so on⸲. But I do not see that beyond this it teaches me that I should ever conclude anything from these various sense perceptions concerning things outside of ourselves, unless the mind has ⌐carefully and⌐ maturely examined them. For it seems to me that it is the business of the mind alone, and not [66] of the being composed of mind and body, to decide the truth of such matters. (83)

Thus, although a star makes no more impression on my eye than the flame of a candle, and there is no real ⸲or positive inclination⸲ ⌐or natural faculty⌐ in me that leads me to believe that it is larger than this flame, nevertheless I have so judged it from infancy for no adequate reason. And although in approaching the flame I feel heat, and even though in approaching it a little too closely I feel pain, there is still no reason that can convince me that there is some quality in the flame similar to this heat, any more than to this pain. I only have reason to believe there is some quality in it, whatever it may be, which arouses in me these feelings of heat or pain.

Similarly, although there are parts of space in which I find nothing that ⌐excites and⌐ affects my senses, I ought not therefore to conclude that they contain no objects. Thus I see that both here and in many other similar cases I am accustomed to ⌐misunderstand and⌐ misconstrue the order of nature, because although these ⌐sensations or⌐ sense perceptions were given to me only to indicate to my mind which objects are useful or harmful to the composite body of which it is a part, and are for that purpose sufficiently clear and distinct, I nevertheless use them as though they were very certain rules by which I could obtain direct information about the essence ⌐and the nature⌐ of external objects, about which they can of course give me no information except very obscurely and confusedly.

In the previous discussion I have already explained sufficiently how it happens, despite the supreme goodness of God, that error occurs in my judgments. One further difficulty, though, presents itself here. This concerns objects which I am taught by nature to seek or avoid and also the internal sensations which she has given me. For it seems to me that I have noticed error here ⌐and thus that I am sometimes directly deceived by my nature⌐—as, for example, when the pleasant taste of some food in which poison has been mixed can induce me to take the poison, and so misleads me. (84) It is nevertheless true that in this case nature ⌐can be excused, for it⌐ only leads me to desire the food in which a pleasant taste is found, and not [67] to desire the poison which is unknown to it. Thus I cannot conclude anything from this except that my nature is not entirely and universally cognizant of all things. And at this there is no reason to be surprised, since man, being of a finite nature, is also restricted to a knowledge of a limited perfection.

But we also make mistakes sufficiently frequently even about matters of which we are directly informed by nature, as happens to sick people when they desire to drink or eat things which ⌐can⌐ ⌐later⌐ harm them. It might be argued here that the reason that they err is that their nature is corrupted. But this does not remove the difficulty, for a sick man is in truth no less the creation of God than is a man in full health, and therefore it is just as inconsistent with the goodness of God for him as for the other to have a ⌐misleading and⌐ faulty nature. A clock, composed of wheels and counterweights, is no less exactly obeying all the laws of nature when it is badly made and does not mark the time correctly than when it completely fulfills the intention of its maker; so also, the human body may be considered as a machine, so built and composed of bones, nerves, muscles, veins, blood, and skin that even if there were no mind in it, it would not cease to move in all the ways that it does at present when it is not moved under the direction of the will, nor consequently with the aid of the mind ⌐, but only by the condition of its organs⌐. I readily recognize that it is quite natural, for example, for this body to suffer dryness in the throat as a result of a dropsical condition, and thus to produce a feeling of thirst in the mind and a consequent disposition on the part of the mind to stimulate the nerves and other parts in the manner requisite for drinking, and so to increase the body's illness ⌐and injure itself⌐. It is just as natural, I say, as it is for it to be beneficially influenced to drink by a similar dryness of the throat, when it is not ill at all. (85)

And although in considering the purpose for which a clock has been intended by its designer, I can say that it is false to its nature when it does not correctly indicate the time, and although in considering the mechanism of the human body in the same way as having been formed ⌐by God⌐ to provide all the customary activities, I have reason to think that it is not functioning according to its nature when its throat is dry and drinking injures its chances of self-preservation, I nevertheless recognize that this last usage of the word "nature" is very different from the other. For the latter is nothing else but an arbitrary appellation [68] which depends entirely on my own idea in comparing a sick man and a poorly made clock, and contrasting them with my idea of a healthy man and a well-made clock; this appellation refers to nothing which is actually found in the objects of which we are talking. On the contrary, by the other usage of the word "nature," I mean something which is actually found in objects and which therefore is not without some truth.

But certainly, although as far as a dropsical body is concerned, it is only an arbitrary appellation to say that its nature is corrupted when, without needing to drink, it still has a dry and arid throat; nevertheless, when we consider the composite body ⌈as a whole⌉—that is to say, the mind ⌈or soul⌉ united with the body—it is not a pure appellation, but ⌈truly⌉ an actual error on the part of nature that it is thirsty when it is very harmful to it to drink. Therefore we must examine how it is that the goodness of God does not prevent man's nature, so considered, from being faulty ⌈and deceptive⌉.

⌈To begin this examination,⌉ (I first take notice here that there is a great difference between the mind and the body, in that the body, from its nature, is always divisible and the mind is completely (86) indivisible.)For in reality, when I consider the mind—that is, when I consider myself in so far as I am only a thinking being—I cannot distinguish any parts, but I ⌈recognize ⌈and⟩ conceive ⟨very clearly⟩⌉ that I am a thing which is ⟨absolutely⟩ unitary and entire. And although the whole mind seems to be united with the whole body, nevertheless when a foot or an arm or some other part ⟨of the body⟩ is amputated, I recognize quite well that nothing has been lost to my mind on that account. Nor can the faculties of willing, perceiving, understanding, and so forth be ⌈any more properly⌉ called parts of the mind, for it is ⟨one and⟩ the same mind which ⌈as a complete unit⌉ wills, perceives, and understands ⌈, and so forth⌉. But just the contrary is the case with corporeal or extended objects, for I cannot imagine any ⌈, however small they might be,⌉ which my mind does not very easily divide into ⌈several⌉ parts, and I consequently recognize these objects to be divisible. This ⟨alone⟩ would suffice to show me that the mind ⌈or soul of man⌉ is altogether different from the body, if I did not already know it sufficiently well for other reasons. [69]

I also take notice that the mind does not receive impressions from all parts of the body directly, but only from the brain, or perhaps even from one of its smallest parts—the one, namely, where the senses in common have their seat. This makes the mind feel the same thing whenever it is in the same condition, even though the other parts of the body can be differently arranged, as is proved by an infinity of experiments which it is not necessary to describe here.

I furthermore notice that the nature of the body is such that no one of its parts can be moved by another part some little distance away without its being possible for it to be moved in the same way by any one of the intermediate parts, even when the more distant part does not act. For example, in the cord A B C D ⌈which is thoroughly stretched⌉, if (87) we pull ⌈and move⌉ the last part D, the first part A will not be moved in any different manner from that in which it could also be moved if we pulled one of the middle parts B or C, while the last part D remained motionless. And in the same way, when I feel pain in my foot, physics teaches me that this sensation is communicated by means of nerves distributed through the foot. When these nerves are pulled in the foot, being stretched like cords from there to the brain, they likewise pull at the same time the ⟨internal⟩ part of the brain ⌈from which they come and⌉ where they terminate, and there produce a certain movement which nature has arranged to make my mind feel pain as though that pain were in my foot. But because these nerves must pass through the leg, the thigh, the loins, the back, and the neck, in order to extend from the foot to the brain, it can happen that even when the nerve endings in the foot are not stimulated, but only some of the ⟨intermediate⟩ parts ⌈located in the loins or the neck⌉, ⟨precisely⟩ the same movements are nevertheless produced in the brain that could be produced there by a wound received in the foot, as a result of which it necessarily follows that the mind feels the same pain ⌐in the foot as though the foot had been wounded⌐. And we must make the same judgment about all our other sense perceptions.

Finally, I notice that since each one of the movements that occurs in the part of the brain from which the mind receives impressions directly can only produce in the mind a single sensation, we cannot ⌐desire or⌐ imagine any better arrangement than that this movement should cause the mind to feel that sensation, of all the sensations the movement is [70] capable of causing, which is most effectively and frequently useful for the preservation of the human body when it is in full health. But experience shows us that all the sensations which nature has given us are such as I have just stated, and therefore there is nothing in their nature which does not show the power and the goodness of ⌐the⌐ God ⌐who has produced them⌐.

Thus, for example, (88) when the nerves of the foot are stimulated violently and more than is usual, their movement, passing through the marrow of the backbone up to the ⌐interior of the⌐ brain, produces there an impression upon the mind which makes the mind feel something—namely, pain as though in the foot—by which the mind is ⌐warned and⌐ stimulated to do whatever it can to remove the cause, taking it to be very ⌐dangerous and⌐ harmful to the foot.

It is true that God could establish the nature of man in such a way that this same brain event would make the mind feel something quite different; for example, it might cause the movement to be felt as though it were in the brain, or in the foot, or else in some other ⌐intermediate⌐ location ⌐between the foot and the brain⌐, or finally it might produce any other feeling ⌐that can exist⌐; but none of those would have contributed so well to the preservation of the body ⌐as that which it does produce⌐.

In the same way, when we need to drink, there results a certain dryness in the throat which affects its nerves and, by means of them, the interior of the brain. This brain event makes the mind feel the sensation of thirst, because under those conditions there is nothing more useful to us than to know that we need to drink for the conservation of our health. And similar reasoning applies to other sensations.

From this it is entirely manifest that, despite the supreme goodness of God, the nature of man, in so far as he is composed of mind and body, cannot escape being sometimes ⌈faulty and⌉ deceptive. For if there is some cause which produces, not in the foot, but in some other part of the nerve which is stretched from the foot to the brain, or even in the brain ⌈itself⌉, the same effect which ordinarily occurs when the foot is injured, we will feel pain as though it were in the foot, and we will naturally be deceived by the sensation. The reason for this is that the same brain event can cause only a single sensation in the mind; and this [71] sensation being much more frequently produced by a cause which wounds the foot than by another acting in a different location, it is much more reasonable (89) that it should always convey to the mind a pain in the foot rather than one in any other part ⌈of the body⌉. And if it happens that sometimes the dryness of the throat does not come in the usual manner from the fact that drinking is necessary for the health of the body, but from some quite contrary cause, as in the case of those afflicted with dropsy, nevertheless it is much better that we should be deceived in that instance than if, on the contrary, we were always deceived when the body was in health; and similarly for the other sensations.

And certainly this consideration is very useful to me, not only so that I can recognize all the errors to which my nature is subject, but also so that I may avoid them or correct them more easily. For knowing that each of my senses conveys truth to me more often than falsehood concerning whatever is useful or harmful to the body, and being almost always able to use several of them to examine the same object, and being in addition able to use my memory to bind and join together present information with what is past, and being able to use my understanding, which has already discovered all the causes of my errors, I should no longer fear to encounter falsity in the objects which are most commonly represented to me by my senses.

And I should reject all the doubts of these last few days as exaggerated and ridiculous, particularly that very general uncertainty about sleep, which I could not distinguish from waking life. For now I find in them a very notable difference, in that our memory can never bind and join our dreams together ⌜one with another and all⌝ with the course of our lives, as it habitually joins together what happens to us when we are awake. And so, in effect, if someone suddenly appeared to me when I was awake and ⟨afterward⟩ disappeared in the same way, as ⌜do images that I see⌝ in my sleep, so that I could not determine where he came from or where he went, it would not be without reason that I would consider it a ghost (90) or a phantom produced in my brain ⌜and similar to those produced there when I sleep⌝, rather than truly a man.

But when I perceive objects in such a way that I distinctly recognize both the place from which they come and the place where they are, as well as the time when they appear to me; and when, without any hiatus, I can relate my perception of them with all the rest of my life, I am entirely certain that I perceive them wakefully and not in sleep. And I should not in any way doubt the truth of these things [72] if, having made use of all my senses, my memory, and my understanding, to examine them, nothing is reported to me by any of them which is inconsistent with what is reported by the others. For, from the fact that God is not a deceiver, it necessarily follows that in this matter I am not deceived.

But because the exigencies of action frequently ⌜oblige us to make decisions and⌝ do not ⌜always⌝ allow us the leisure to examine these things with sufficient care, we must admit that human life is very often subject to error in particular matters; and we must in the end recognize the infirmity ⌜and weakness⌝ of our nature.